GW01110613

The Dubliner 100 Best Restaurants 2003
by Domini Kemp and Trevor White.
Photography and design by Joanne Murphy.

First edition, published August 2003.
ISBN 0-9542188-1-7

The Dubliner

Published by *The Dubliner* Magazine
23 Wicklow Street, Dublin 2.
Telephone 01 635 9822 *email* dining@thedubliner.ie

All rights reserved. No part of this publication may be reproduced, without the prior permission of the publishers. While every care has been taken to ensure accuracy throughout this book, the publishers cannot be held responsible for any errors or omissions.
All contents ©Dubliner Media Ltd. 2003

Contents

Foreword	1
Introduction	2
The 100 Best Restaurants	6
Index	134
Maps	136

Page no.

A little help

First line of Address
Second line of Address
Telephone, Email and Website

Don't go looking for rankings. There aren't any. Rather, this book showcases 100 restaurants in the city and county of Dublin that deserve your business. They are listed in alphabetical order. At the bottom of each entry, a bar across the page lists the postal district and the type of food you can expect to eat in the restaurant. Except where specified, expect to pay more for a meal in Dublin than you would in a European town renowned for its cooking. There are many reasons for this, including the high cost of imported produce and exorbitant rates of VAT on food and drink. One cannot simply lament the greed of Irish restaurateurs. Finally, there is an index and a map at the back of this book.

Expensive   *Cheap*   *New Entry*

1 Type of Restaurant

Foreword

Vina Santa Rita has a long association with Ireland, dating back to when Chile's national hero, the Irishman Bernardo O'Higgins, used the cellars of Casa Real to hide with 120 of his men from the Spanish Imperial forces. Those cellars are still used to store South America's finest wines.

Gilbeys has an equally proud history. The company set up offices in 1858 on Sackville Street, which is now O'Connell Street, and it prospered through times when the capital was no vinous paradise.

In truth, there are two Dublins now. The first one "holds my mind," as Louis MacNeice put it, "with her seedy elegance, with her gentle veils of rain and all her ghosts that hide behind her Georgian facades." The second is unwieldy, ambitious, a new and better town which has not found its feet.

Dublin's restaurants are one of the most obvious examples of changes sweeping the city. Hence the need for a reliable guide. Each month, thousands of people read what Domini Kemp and Trevor White have to say about dining in Dublin. Irreverent, informed and often amusing, their reviews are for people who love eating out, and we are delighted to associate Santa Rita with the definitive guide to the best dining the capital has to offer. I hope you enjoy using the guide – and happy eating!

Fergal Downey
Gilbeys Wines

Introduction

The French have their snails. The English love roast beef. The Belgians suck on mussels. Here in Ireland, our national dish is the Doner Kebab. We have no culinary tradition and, with a couple of exceptions – bacon and cabbage, the wretched spud – we have no indigenous cuisine. When we go out to a restaurant, we are more likely to order chicken Kiev or spaghetti Bolognaise than anything the Irish dreamed up. Neither inspire much hope.

For such a nation of bitchy toads, we are remarkably slow to complain when a meal is disappointing. And let's face it: there's a lot to moan about. Even in a good Irish restaurant, nobody wants to take responsibility. The chef is preening himself on television. The menu is in a foreign language. The prices are blamed on Charlie McCreevy, the interior was designed by the owner's wife and the waiter would rather be in front of a camera.

It should be stressed that these comments only apply to the locals. Many of Dublin's better restaurants are managed or owned by foreigners. This opinion will offend those dear bigots who moan about "staff who can't speak English," but in truth we have much to learn from immigrants.

It is possible to eat well in Dublin, although you have to be careful about how and where you spend your money. That's where this little book comes in. We don't think that all 100 restaurants will be around this time next year – nine of last year's crop have closed – and we certainly don't pretend that all are brilliant (how small that book would be). But we have eaten in these restaurants, and none of them made us sick.

High praise? Hardly. If you want to read press releases, you're in the wrong place. We write for the benefit of punters, and not for the vanity of chefs. That's why they're so rude to us. It's also why you kept the first edition of this book on the best-seller list for six months. Thank you.

We hope this second edition is equally useful. If you have any quibbles or suggestions about the book or any of these reviews, please don't hesitate to contact us at *The Dubliner* magazine. Equally, if you don't rate our reviews, by all means have a go yourself. Each month we print a reader's review of a meal in a Dublin restaurant. Consider it a chance to spread good news – or call it just deserts.

Domini Kemp and Trevor White
August 2003

ONE GREAT IRISHMAN FACED
SWORD, CAVALRY AND CANNON
TO LIBERATE OUR WINES.

ALL YOU HAVE TO DO IS TACKLE THIS:

Defeated after a long hard day's battle, Bernardo O'Higgins and 120 of his rebels did what many a weary office trooper has done after him.

They sought refuge in our cellars.

A fact now commemorated by Santa Rita's "120" range of fine wines.

Because it was in our cellars over a relaxing red or a reviving white that O'Higgins and his 120 men plotted, planned and conspired their comeback.

A comeback that would see the illegitimate son of an Irish colonial officer and a local belle go on to lead Chile. Quite a feat. And one we would like to credit to the power of our wines.

As they too have gone on to become world class leaders, picking up quite a few decorations en route.

However, it did take a few years and a number of other factors before O'Higgins and his men could lay down their swords and lift their glasses to independence.

So next time you grapple with a cork-screw, think of that great Irishman facing sword, cavalry and cannon.

Then raise a glass of Santa Rita to his fight for Chilean freedom.

And - dare we say - your freedom to chill.

PURVEYORS OF PLEASURE
— Since 1880 —
WWW.THEWINEROOM.IE

101 Talbot

100-102 Talbot Street
Dublin 1
t 874 5011

Smug southsiders never shut up about Talbot 101. That's because it's on the northside – we are startled to find a decent restaurant on this side of the Liffey. Consistency and value are the buzzwords, but don't go looking for lavish comfort: this 12 year-old is always packed, and it isn't the Four Seasons. An unpretentious gem, 101 offers good food with stellar service and owners – husband and wife team Pascal and Margaret – who take the veggie punter seriously (40% of the menu is vegan friendly). Fresh pastas, salads and roasts are usually delicious. Don't leave without trying the chocolate and hazelnut cake. The menu changes weekly, and is usually a model of invention. The service is cheerful rather than formal, but 101 is not about *haute cuisine*. It's a damn shame they don't open for lunch anymore.

Cheap & Cheerful

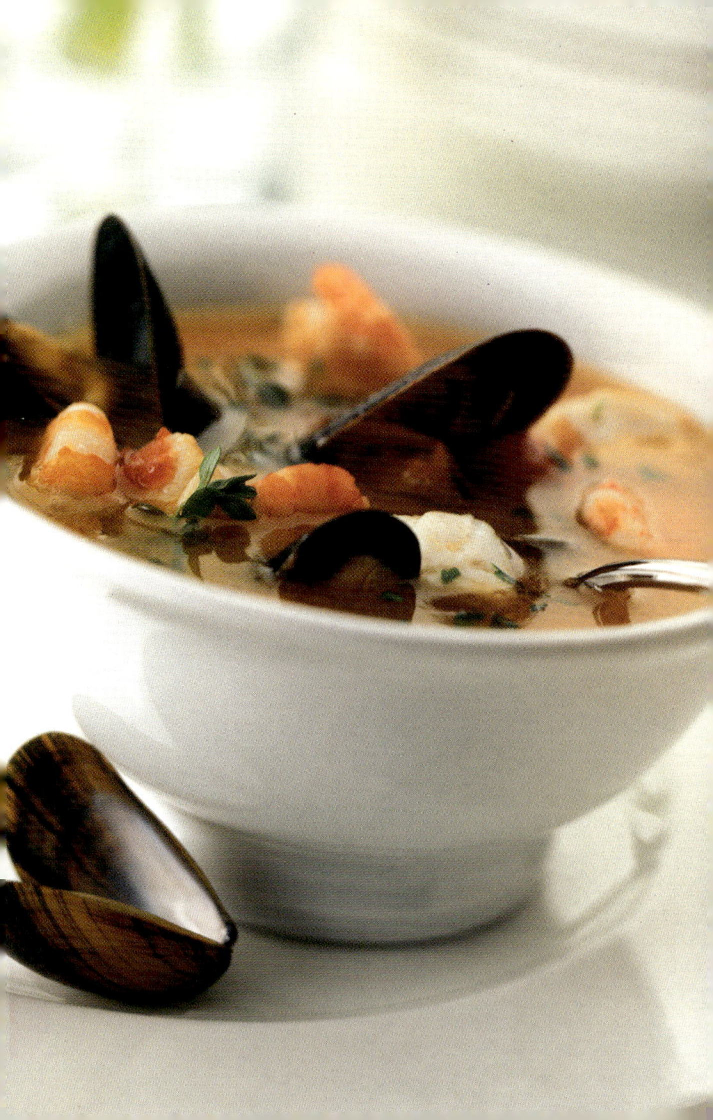

Alilang

102 Parnell Street
Dublin 1
t 814 6814

In North Korea they like to build nuclear weapons and in South Korea they like to eat dogs. The menu at Alilang is ten pages long, and there's not a single mention of dog in the whole thing. Marinated chicken stomach, yes; dried jellyfish, yes, but Dalmatian, no. The furniture is all cheap farmhouse pine and set into the middle of each table is a round metal plate, connected to the gas. A gang of young Koreans were cooking up strips of marinated beef on a saucepan lid, with a lot of enthusiasm and not much finesse. When our raw cuttlefish with cucumber (€11.80) arrived, we got equally excited. Strips of toothsome squid and splinters of spring onions, peppers and ginger swam in a lake of fiery red sauce. These chillies are particularly hot – beware. The waiter told us that Korean wine is like vodka and then laughed for a very long time. We stuck to green tea, which is on the house.

Korean

Aqua

1 West Pier, Howth
County Dublin
t 832 0690
w www.aqua.ie

Spring 2003. It's a lazy Sunday morning and we've just walked out to the end of the pier. There's a chill, but the sun is out. A lone busker blows trumpet, sound sails in the wind and suddenly Howth feels ever-so-slightly chic. Across the road and up the stairs to Aqua, which is surrounded by water on three sides (it used to be Howth Yacht Club). A warm welcome, roaring fire. Glass of sherry, pint for him. Into the dining room, and more live jazz. The seafood chowder is probably Dublin's finest, and my John Dory with garlic, olives and peppers is just right. Instead of dessert I demand another bowl of chowder. The waiter smiles and says "Sure. You're not the first." Good food, wonderful views, excellent service: at €26 for Sunday lunch it doesn't come cheap, but Aqua deserves your business.

Seafood CD

Avoca

11-13 Suffolk Street
Dublin 2
t *672 6019*
w *www.avoca.ie*

Decades after the first branch opened, Avoca is still a major hit with the botox-beauties of South County Dublin. Watch them *shlep* up the stairs, laden down with bags full of Mexican cardigans and a bar of Belgian chocolate for mum. They look visibly relieved to have spent a small fortune on acquiring the Avoca lifestyle; and that's truly what it is. With an airy top-floor café and the food hall in the basement, this city-centre outpost feels like an Irish General Trading Company. When you spend money here, you're buying into a dream. Start with the smoked trout, smoked tuna and dill paté (€8.95). Then have the Tuscan salad of rocket, parmesan shavings and crisp Parma ham (€12.95). Wash it down with a glass of real orange juice (€2.50). Yes, this is Avoca-Lite for townies, but so what? Upbeat, bright and outrageously healthy, it's just like a trip to the real Avoca – minus Sunday drivers.

Modern Irish

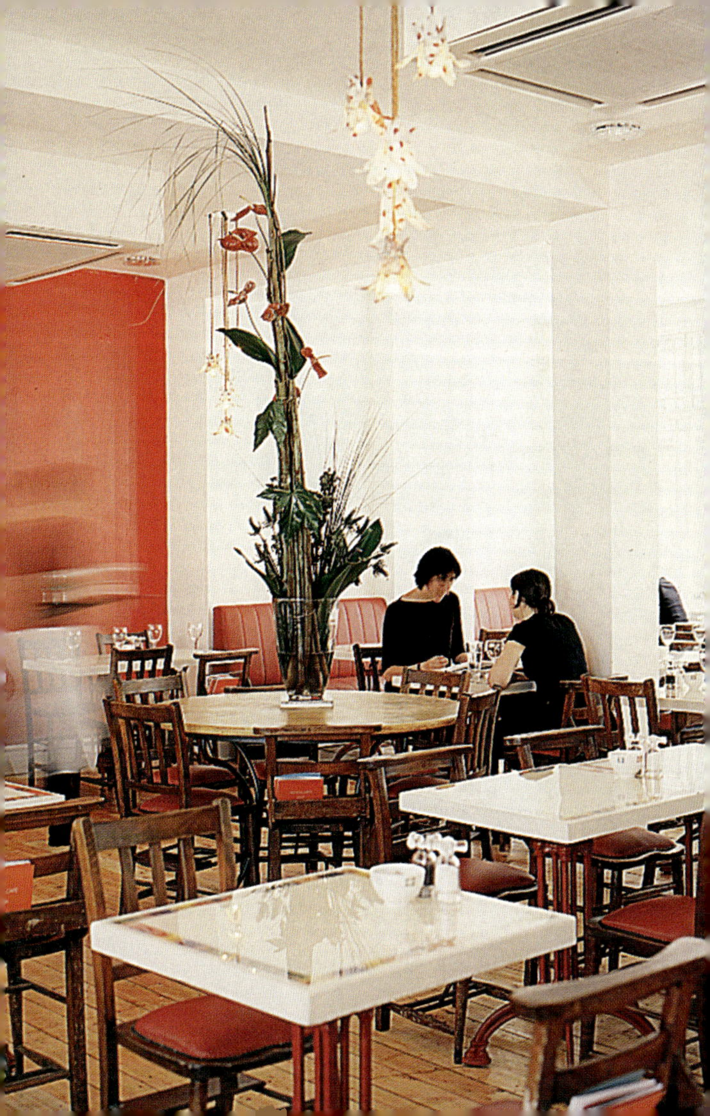

Ar Vicoletto

5 Crow Street, Temple Bar
Dublin 2
t 670 8662

Luigi Santoro opened the Steps of Rome with his beautiful wife before leaving them both for a waitress. These days you'll find him here in Temple Bar – or around the corner, at his pizzeria on Parliament Street, Ciao Bella Roma. We prefer Ar Vicoletto, which is nothing if not authentic. It is small, usually full of smoke and not particularly comfortable. Neither Luigi, the chef nor the staff speak much English, which is comical or maddening, depending on your mood. Start with the bresaola (€11.36) and follow it with rigatone con melanzone (€11.36) or the spaghetti al frutti di mare (€13.90). The food is never spectacular and you'll probably end up sitting on top of your neighbours, but at least there is plenty of atmosphere – unlike many (so-called) restaurants in Temple Bar. Hats off, then, to the bold Luigi.

Italian

Aya

Clarendon Street, Dublin 2
t 677 1544 e mail@aya.ie
w www.aya.ie

Customers: middle aged women and colleen brats who watch too much *Sex & the City*. Nice staff in cutesy uniforms, clean premises. Quite a slick operation – a mini-Japanese empire, if you will. The pre-packaged sushi boxes are bland, so one cannot be blamed for forgetting how pleasant the restaurant can be. Our beef tataki (€8.90) was seared on the outside and served blue (yes, that's less than rare) in a good soy, sesame and spring onion dressing. We also had miso soup (€3) and a whole smorgasbord of norimaki, sushi and hand rolls with some very nice hamachi. It's not especially cheap, but if you are broke, remember their twilight-deals at the conveyer-belt sushi bar (yawn). We had a half-bottle of Gewurtztraminer and copious amounts of green tea. Finish the bottle, close your eyes and pretend you're in Nobu.

Japanese

Il Baccaro

Meeting House Square, Temple Bar
Dublin 2
t 671 4597

We could bang on about the new chef and the departure of their best looking waitress, but in truth, nothing has changed in this basement bistro, which is the only cheap and cheerful thing about Temple Bar. Our advice in 2002 still rings true: "order plenty of starters, loads of wine (stay away from the house red) and be very careful about picking main courses." Does that sound risky? Live a little and order the grilled mushrooms with pesto, the bresaola, the antipasti, caponata and grilled focaccia. Waiters were less surly than last year (almost flirty), which made the evening a lot nicer. Get this: if you go with a gang of Italians, you get unchartered magic (a bit like off-piste skiing). The pasta dishes came out rich, authentic and smiles were freely traded. Italian pals are not obligatory – go with a Paddy and follow our guidelines.

Italian

Bad Ass Café

9-11 Crown Alley, Temple Bar
Dublin 2
t 671 2596

"Young pups love the Bad Ass," said *The Dubliner* columnist Helen Lucy Burke in 1988. Back then, the total bill for six people came to £39.18, and those lovely people at Temple Bar Properties had yet to cast their super-pub spell. "It is a very good place," wrote HLB, "if you think in terms of what kids enjoy." Sinead O'Connor doesn't work here anymore, and the prices have gone up – not by much – but the Bad Ass remains a monument to the ultra-cheesy 1980s. The delivery system still whizzes along on overhead wires, the pizzas are still unremarkable, fathers still admire the staff and you'll still hear Annie Lennox moaning on the stereo. For children, nostalgia junkies and 30-somethings who haven't got around to growing up yet. P.S. The fact that the Bad Ass merits inclusion on a list of the city's 100 best restaurants tells its own sorry tale.

Bang

11 Merrion Row
Dublin 2
t 676 0898
w www.bangrestaurant.com

This restaurant is so popular that people arrive for dinner at 11pm on a week-night. None are over 35, and most of them are bored of modelling. We prefer Bang when it's a bit quieter and the kitchen is able to cope. Try the gorgeous scallops with pancetta and mousseline potatoes, a seared tuna salad, the bangers and mash or the baked seabass with fragrant rice. Identical twins Chris and Simon Stokes are the beautiful boys who own this little machine. They also own a pub called The Clarendon, which is great for fish and chips at lunch. Bang's prime location, handsome staff and fine food are all good for business, which means you'll probably have to wait for a table, even if you booked it last month. Cranky customers resent this policy. Try to leave them at home.

Modern European

Bangkok Café

106 Parnell Street
Dublin 1
t 878 6618

This Thai café is the sort of place that John McKenna loves. It's small, dirty and dark. The location could not be more intimidating: behind a door (that is always locked) in an area of town that needs more than the Gate to entice smart Dubliners. Still, it's worth a gamble. Mo Hennessy's Thai cooking is assured, exotic. But do make sure that Mo is in the kitchen, and not at her place in the country. Try the Bangkok selection, a great appetiser combo, with succulent satay chicken and fishcakes. Follow up with some Choo Choo grilled chicken, marinated in garlic and chilli sauce (€12.95). Then you'll understand why gourmet gurus rave about this peculiar little place. By the way, BC is a perfect spot for dates: guys like the prices and dig doing the wrong side of town. Girls – wiser – love the food. Check it out.

Thai

Beaufield Mews

Woodlands Avenue, Stillorgan
County Dublin
t 288 0375
w www.beaufieldmews.com

This place reminds me of Hunter's hotel. Hunting prints, dark wood and charming gardens lend further cred to my *déja vu* theory. Unlike Hunter's, everything here is for sale. One o'clock on Sunday: the dining room is throbbing. Large families celebrate birthdays and wedding anniversaries of the gold or silver variety. Norma Smurfit is entertaining, and Seamus Brennan sulks. We order in the bar, and moments later, our starters have appeared. Joining them, we crowd around a table that is slightly too low and cramped. Ordering, I forgot a valuable lesson from my Hunter's days. If it's Sunday lunch, order the roast, and ignore the veggie option. I had melon in a winterberry coulis followed by roasted, stuffed peppers. Both were disappointing. His lordship had delicious chicken liver paté and the best roast pork I've tasted in ages... right beside me. Men are so inconsiderate.

CD Traditional Irish

Berkeley Room

Berkeley Court Hotel, Lansdowne Road
Dublin 4
☏ 665 3271

A new German chef, Volker Mareck, has joined the team, but this swanky steakhouse in the Berkeley Court still reeks of old-Dublin. It is the sort of place where schemes are hatched, mischief ensues and before you know it, you've drunk half a bottle of brandy. The food is better than your ideas, and there's a new table d'hote menu (€42). Try the Dublin Bay prawns, flamed and served with diced pears, cream and Calvados (€32) and follow it with oak smoked rack of lamb on a ragout of black eye and kidney beans, polenta cake and jus flavoured with fig vinegar. Sunday lunch is particularly good fun; watch political icons do battle with their children, and nouveau stars attempt to use a fish knife. All very amusing – but cheap? No way, sweetie.

Traditional Irish

Bijou

47 Highfield Road, Rathgar
Dublin 6
t 496 1518 e bijourestaurant@eircom.net

It's true – us foodies dig our graves with our teeth. Out we go, night after night, foraging for food that merits applause. That air of resignation accompanied our last trip to Bijou, on a cold, damp summer evening. It was nearly empty when we arrived, which didn't help matters. And the owners are proud of the "cheesy background music." But we enjoyed our dinner. The service was grand, and the food – well, it wasn't as memorable as it used to be, but by Dublin standards it was worth the trek. Standout starter was the seared lamb kidneys (€8.25) while the best of the mains was the seared loin of veal with crushed herb baby potatoes, shallot coulis and roasted flat top mushrooms (€25.35). Don't leave without trying the homemade chocolate fudge gateau (€6.50). Expensive enough, but then, Rathgar is getting rather grand these days. By the way, Linda and Mark Smith also own the Deli Boutique down the road.

Modern Irish

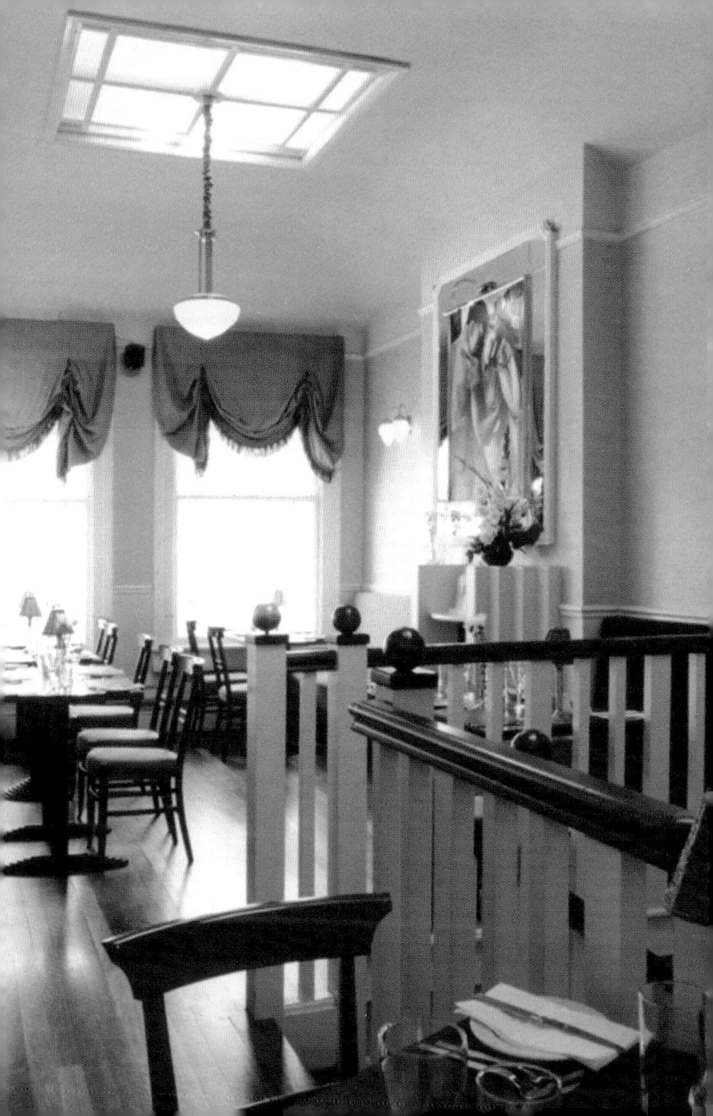

Bistro One

3 Brighton Road, Foxrock Village
Dublin 18
t 289 7711

They say that cockroaches and socialites are the only people who can stay up all night and eat anything. You'll see plenty of the latter at this fashionable first floor bistro, which is the sort of place where your fellow diners have perfect hair, expensive teeth and voices that could crack a wine glass at 30 paces. *Image* Publisher Kevin Kelly famously coined the term Foxrock Fanny to describe this abominable breed. Still, the food is good. We usually start with the Bistro One salad with pancetta, rocket and pine nuts (€7) and follow it with either the roast crispy duck in sage and shallot stuffing (€23) or the fish and chips (€17). Yes, these aren't bistro prices, the wine list is dreary and there's an obligatory 10% service charge. But despite all that, we like Bistro One. Bring your snobby cow of a godmother.

Modern European

The Bistro

4/5 Castle Market
Dublin 2
t 671 5430

One of us fought to get Grogan's pub into this book. It is the perfect place to bunk off work on a rainy day – legendary pints of Guinness, cosy atmosphere, lovely staff and great toasted sandwiches. If the sun comes out and you're still there, cross the road to the Bistro, where you can sit oustide and continue your discussion on the state of the nation. You'll have to order food, and the service is sometimes sloppy, but on a warm evening there is something "very continental" about this little strip of Dublin reborn. The menu changes regularly. Pastas are good, not outstanding. Salads (Caesar, Caprese, spinach and bacon with balsamic dressing) are fine. At dinner, the mains can be very pricey considering the calibre of grub. Fillet of beef with chips and béarnaise was just not good enough for €28.50. Lunch is better value.

World

Bleu Bistro

Joshua House, Dawson Street
Dublin 2
t 676 7015

Okay, let's get this straight. Eamon O'Reilly is not the new *enfant terrible*. He's slightly chubby, improbably gifted and has opened a string of trendy eateries - nice art too - in record time, but this doesn't mean that Eamon is about to do a Conrad. Mind you, one of his new babies, Pacific, has changed hands already, which doesn't inspire a great deal of confidence. O'Reilly's latest offering is quite smart. Very Uptown location - beside the Mansion House and across the road from the crumbling RIAC. It is not particularly expensive. The interior is elegant. We like those plate glass windows (mind you, there are too many tables for a room of this size). The food started off great. It's still not bad. Start with the salmon creme brulée, cucumber pickle and melba toast (€7.95). To follow, have the omelette Arnold Bennett with smoked haddock (€14.95). Service is wobbly.

2 French

Bon Appetit

9 St James Terrace, Malahide
County Dublin
t *845 0314* ***e*** *info@bonappetit.ie*

Are you a southside snob? If fine claret is your thing and you like things classical rather than contemporary, this comfortable old restaurant is a good reason to go Northside. Michael Douglas, Alex Ferguson and CJ Haughey have all worshipped at the temple of Monaghan man Patsy McGuirk. Why? "Modern" Irish fare. Stick to fishy classics like Carlingford oysters, Dublin Bay prawns, monkfish with prawns, roast turbot and grilled Dover sole on the bone. Meat and game also put in an appearance; roast crispy duckling, fillet steak. Prices are reasonable, given the rich ambience: about €10 for starters, €25 for mains. An extensive wine list and superb service are the real reasons for making this pilgrimage – unless, of course, you live locally, in which case Patsy is a hero of sorts, and a "genuine" culinary giant.

Traditional Irish | CD

The Brewery Bar

Fifth Floor, Guinness Storehouse
St James' Gate, Dublin 8
t 408 4800
w www.guinness-storehouse.com

Englishman Mark Poulton-Smyth makes great Irish food in a bar that shuts before all others (10pm). That the bar is owned by Guinness seems downright odd, but heck we're all so responsible now. If you have to show visitors around the city, dump them in the Storehouse. Sneak off to lunch in the Brewery Bar on the fifth floor, where you can dissect their irritating habits – "to think, that bitch is my cousin" – and tuck into classic Irish fare at surprisingly reasonable prices. The Limerick glazed bacon and buttered kale served with champ potatoes (€9.90) is good, but this being Rome, you really have to try the beef and Guinness stew with parsnip crisps (€9.80). After lunch, go up to the Gravity Bar and look with awe upon the city that you call home. Give thanks for being yourself – not your stupid cousin – and reflect on the fact that Dublin is really quite pretty.

Modern Irish

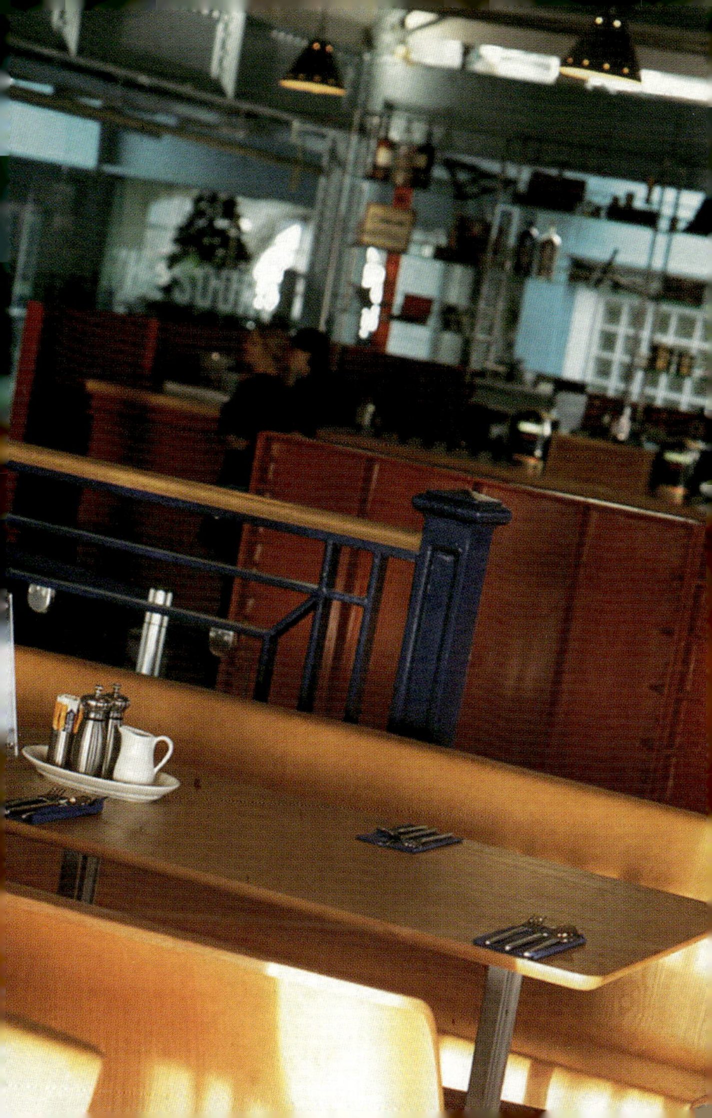

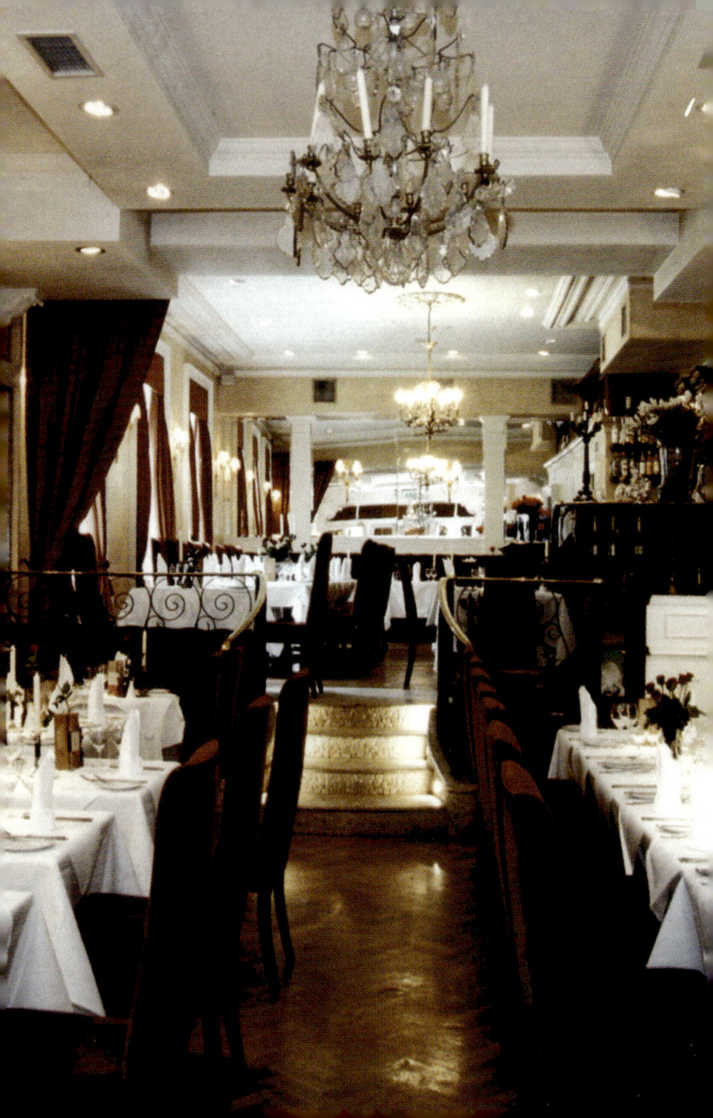

Brownes Brasserie 29

22 St Stephens Green
Dublin 2
t 638 3939 e info@brownesdublin.com
w www.brownesdublin.com

With its handsome interior and kind lighting, Browne's has plenty of atmosphere – but is it "the most romantic establishment in the British Isles"? Not quite. We like it nonetheless. Lawyers come for lunch and stay all afternoon – the naughty retire upstairs, to a bed once used by Marilyn Monroe (is that romantic?). Last week the food was by no means outstanding, but no major problems. The people at the table beside us were delightfully indiscreet (a bunch of lads from *and on* Foreign Affairs). The two course lunch menu is good value at €20. A Caesar salad was over-dressed but the cod special – in a kind of Asian seafood sauce – compensated. Best dish on the menu is the roast fillet of home smoked salmon with spring onion mash, red wine and black mustard seed sauce. Service was excellent. By the way, owner Barry Canny is about to open a very smart wine bar down the road.

Formal 2

Café Bar Deli

12-13 South Great Georges Street
Dublin 2
t 677 1646

This is one of our favourite spots for cheap lunch or dinner in town. Alas we're not alone. Best to ignore the other customers, who are either a. greasy students or b. brain-dead musicians (have you ever noticed that musicians sound clever when they're talking about music – and nothing else?). Grab yourself a banquette, order garlic pizzette, a bowl of old-fashioned spaghetti Bolognaise and a pint of Erdinger (total price €16.89). Note how courteous and charming the staff are. Manager Neil Rooney has the largest smile in Europe. Eat and drink. Reflect on the astonishing success of Jay Bourke and Eoin Foyle – they also own the Globe, RíRá and Eden – who have basically created a new template for city living. They also made George's Street fashionable once again. Raise a glass to this bold new emblem of Dublin re-born – a Bewleys for the 21st century.

World

Captain Americas

44 Grafton Street
Dublin 2
t 671 5266 e bookings@captainamericas.com
w www.captainamericas.com

Great restaurants, said Frederic Raphael, are nothing but mouth-brothels. With that in mind, we made room this year for an aging tart. Property developer Mark Kavanagh – who went on to build the IFSC – opened this bare-chested homage to American rawk in 1971. Chris de Burgh famously started out playing to bemused Irish audiences in Captain A's, before discovering that people in Luxembourg genuinely like his music. It is still technically the only bar on Grafton street, and it also houses a "rock and roll museum." But such bland statistics do not do justice to the deeply ironic thrill of dining in Dublin's first truly tacky restaurant. Kids and celebrities love the burgers, which are at least cheap. Everyone else just chuckles: at the stars, the guitars and the "fact" that people get engaged in the booths. We love you, Captain A.

World 2

La Cave

28 South Anne Street
Dublin 2
t 679 4409
w www.lacavewinebar.com

Your mother wouldn't like La Cave – which doesn't mean it's bad. But it really is a late night "wine" bar, down a seedy flight of stairs into a hot, dark room. Indeed with its moody lighting, fading lustre and more than a hint of intrigue, it feels like a chic ex-pat hangout in colonial Africa. There's a long wine-list, from affordable house wines by the glass or bottle (around €15) to triple-figure clarets. Bubbly blonde Trudi Rothwell is a grand hostess. Reasonable Gallic cuisine: either a four-course table d'hote (€27.90) or à la carte, as well as late-night snacks. Try the baked goat's cheese salad (€6). Follow it with the mushroom ravioli, truffle oil and parmesan shavings (€13.90) – but do ask for extra truffle oil! – or the chicken couscous (€15.15). La Cave is a smart venue for first dates – the lighting is kind – and a quiet tipple here is a fine way to end the evening when you're not quite drunk enough for Joy's.

French

Cavistons

59 Glasthule Road, Sandycove
County Dublin
t 280 9120 e info@cavistons.ie
w www.cavistons.com

We sat beside Michael O'Leary and his fiancée last Saturday. He made the smart decision – as usual – to book for the last of three sittings for lunch. Peter Caviston still refuses to open this tiny little place for dinner. Next door to his painfully fashionable deli and fish shop, you will rub shoulders (literally) with Southside royalty and sundry foodies. Most of the customers know Peter, and his ebullient personality is evident elsewhere too: the cooking is confident, unashamedly simple and full of flavour. "Whatever comes in on the day, we sell on the day," says the boss. Now six years old, it's almost impossible to get a table without a reservation – unless, that is, you're a regular, like Maeve Binchy and Tim Pat Coogan. Start with the chowder, or the whole prawns á la plancha. Follow with half a lobster or black sole on the bone. What's your secret, Peter? "Let the fish do the talking." Indeed.

Seafood CD

The Cedar Tree

11a St Andrew Street
Dublin 2
t 677 2121

After a disappointing first experience, we now like this buzzy Lebanese place, which is better than most of the restaurants in the centre of town. A smiling gentleman (and the smile feels genuine) greets you, seats you, takes you through the menu. When the food arrives he explains every dish with such pride and relish that you know it's going to be good. The Cedar Tree has career waiters and you can tell the difference; in other words, you don't get the impression that the staff would rather be on-stage. The dining room is also a winner: a cosy basement, nicely lit, with inlaid mahogany tables. Order one of the set menus (around €35) with things like hummous, tabbouleh, lamb on a skewer, aubergine paste – all reasonable fare, served with pitta bread. At this price I can think of few better places for groups of four to eight people. It's also quite romantic, thus worth remembering for dates with exotic strangers.

2 Lebanese

The Dubliner

"IRELAND'S BEST MAGAZINE"

The Cellar

Merrion Hotel, Merrion Street
Dublin 2
t 603 0630 e info@merrionhotel.com
w www.merrionhotel.com

This is Mornington's after plastic surgery. Tacky peach and pink shades are now beige stone, white walls and lots of art. The Cellar Bar is still open for pub grub, but on Sunday we were forced to upgrade to the restaurant. No problem, except that the dining room was rather bright – not exactly hangover-friendly. Still, they sure give good brunch. There is a fried egg with wild mushrooms on toast (€6), plum tomato and pesto gallette with arugula (€6) and some spinach salad with Roquefort and French fries. You can also have scrambled eggs with smoked salmon (€14), or a fillet of smoked haddock with champ and grain mustard sauce (€13.50). The dinner menu looks good, and if the usual Merrion standards are applied, the Cellar will hold its own. That is no mean feat, when you consider the company it keeps; Restaurant Patrick Guilbaud is in the same building.

Modern Irish

Chai Yo

100 Lower Baggot Street
Dublin 2
t 676 7652

We like this spot, despite initial resentment. You know the vibe: creepy restaurant shuts down and re-emerges as yet another ethnic temple. Lots of cheap chicken and meat, chilli and soy sauce plus a good splash of fish sauce. Oooh, and a bit of Thai basil because we're so damn exotic these days. Chai Yo is a bit more fun – teppan-yaki tables on one floor (think a Thai Tom Cruise in *Cocktail*, but with food, silly) and regular Thai/Chinese restaurant below. Tom Yam soup (€6) was well seasoned. Great sticky chicken yakatori for €6. Avocado roll is best value norimaki in town – two portions of that at €5 each will stuff you full of rice. Tori Katsu (€15.50) was a bit dry and eggy, but tasty enough when drenched with soy sauce. We were serenaded by a Thai boy band – Louis Walsh would love them – in the middle of a lovers' tiff. It was well-timed or extraordinarily inappropriate, depending on who tells the story.

Chapter One

18/19 Parnell Square
Dublin 1
t 873 2266 e info@chapteronerestaurant.com
w www.chapteronerestaurant.com

This is Domini's favourite restaurant. She's not alone. If you're serious about good food and you want a fine-dining experience that is reasonably priced and more casual than Guilbauds, this is where you go. They've revamped the restaurant – at last the loos are cute – so this fine old dining room beneath the Writers' Museum now offers ancient style and modern comfort. Owner Ross Lewis has given some of the kitchen-reins to Garret Byrne, formerly of Bruno's on Kildare Street, where we had some excellent dinners under his watch. Try the foie gras, fried egg and black pudding. The charcuterie trolley is legendary. And keep an ear on your neighbours' table. Only four types of people eat at Chapter One: actors, journalists, lawyers and people who sleep with them. All have stories to tell.

1 Formal

China-Sichuan

4 Lower Kilmacud Road, Stillorgan
County Dublin
t 288 4817

We asked David and Julie Hui to tell us what makes their restaurant special. "Nothing really, we're just doing the same thing, serving the same food consistently for the last 19 years." On that basis you might assume that China-Sichuan is all same-same, as generic and tasteless as a bad spring roll. The exterior doesn't help – a row of old shops in Stillorgan, the rich man's answer to Kimmage. Inside, the restaurant is equally drab. But the food is good. Try the shredded pork in garlic sauce, the smoked duck with pancakes (€20.32) or whole black sole in a yellow bean sauce (€20.95). Young pretenders like Wong's and Kites are trying to convince us that Chinese food should be taken seriously. China-Sichuan settled that score a long time ago. What a shame it doesn't feel vaguely glamorous; if this were a beauty contest, both young rivals would win hands down.

Chinese | CD

The Chili Club

1 Anne's Lane
Dublin 2
t 677 3721

It's easy to forget about this discreet little place up a lane at the back of super-pub central. Don't. There's an integrity about Ireland's first Thai restaurant (now ten years old) that is rare enough in town. Maybe it's the cooking itself, which is consistently good – thanks to fresh ingredients and a sensitive hand at the hob – or maybe it's the hush-hush atmosphere. Either way, the Chili Club is a fine spot for a cheapish lunch on a rainy day with someone who is either too notorious or too ugly for public consumption. Our favourite dishes include the Chili Club selection for two people (€12.50) and the gaeng kari gai, a yellow curry chicken with coconut milk (€15.50). Beware of the service, which is necessarily obtrusive: it's such a small room that you can't help feeling snooped on by staff who are simply being attentive. And yes, that *is* Andrea Corr.

Thai

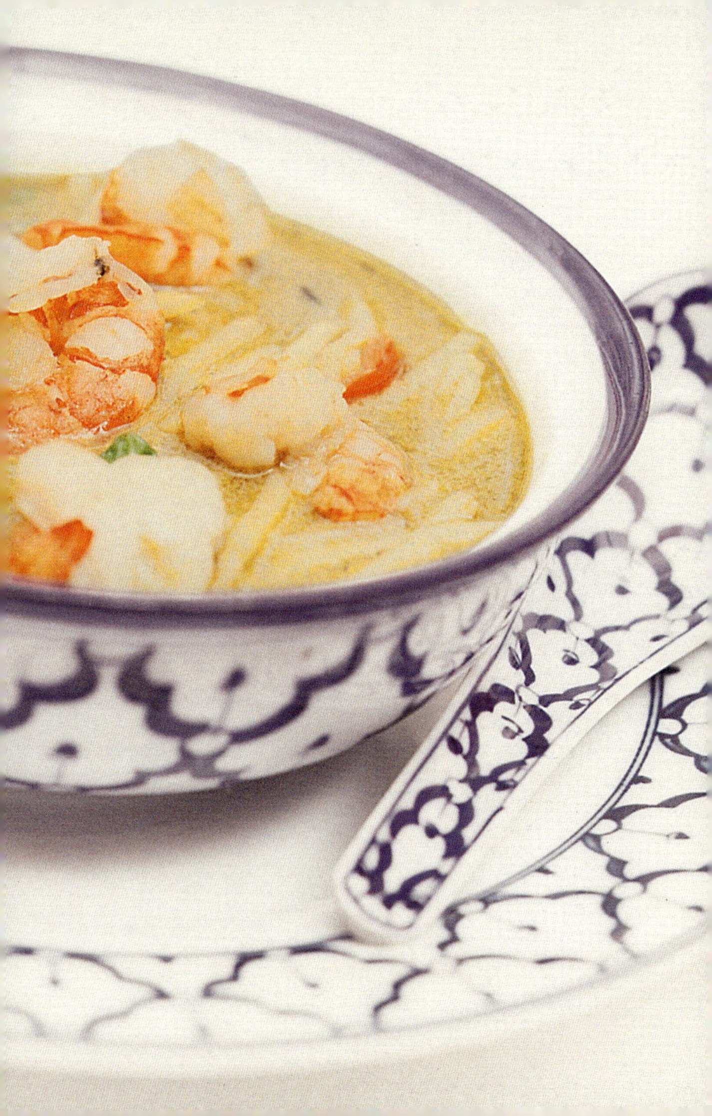

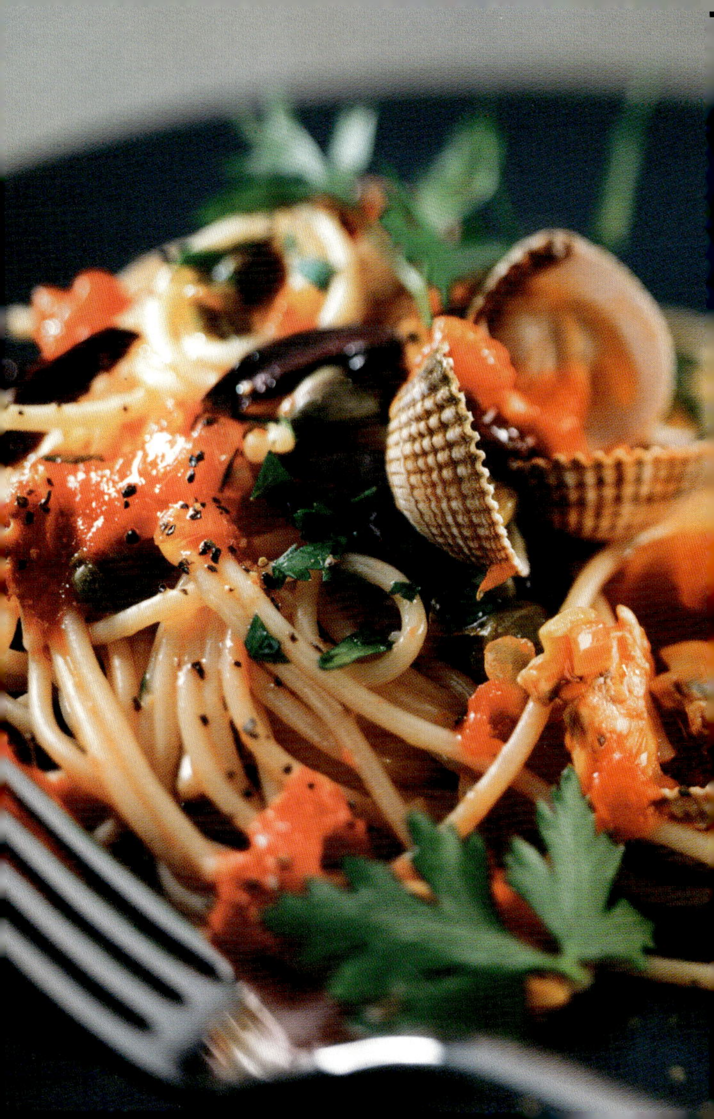

La Corte

Powerscourt Townhouse Centre
South William Street, Dublin 2
t 633 4477

Jo Brand says she wouldn't give someone her last Rolo if they were in a diabetic coma. You've got to love people who take food that seriously. But would she eat lunch in the middle of a glorified shopping centre? We do it all the time. Stefano Crescenzi and David Izzo's balcony restaurant at the top of the Powerscourt Townhouse is a worthy successor to all the crap restaurants that have tried and failed to stay the course in this great old building. Go for lunch with someone who values good cooking over ambience. Share the bruschetta and the Caprese salad to start. Then have tagliatelle with mushrooms, or one of the pasta specials – they are always good. We love the gnocchi funghi e rughetta (€7.50). Finish with coffee – slap, bang – and don't forget to flirt with the waiters. All wink and muscle, hardly any English, they are the real deal and we can't get enough of them.

Italian 2

D One

North Wall Quay
Dublin 1
t 856 1622

We reviewed a long, boozy lunch in this box-in-the-docks last spring. Owners Cian Mooney and Chris Bailie got in touch to point out that we didn't even mention the food. We were tempted to say that AA Gill never does either, but hey, at least the man can write. Anyway, we went back to D One for dinner, and came away quietly impressed. An ultra-modern bungalow – plate glass windows, modern minimalist furnishings – at dusk it really feels chic. A starter portion of smoked haddock risotto with sun-dried tomatoes, scallions, lime crème fraiche and parmesan (€9.50) was the highlight of the evening, while fish and chips (€13.80) pleased a hungry teen. If you fancy a decent curry without the wailing cat, try the lamb jalfrezi with coriander rice and poppadoms (€15.80). Efficient, cheerful service, sensible prices and lots of local parking lend further charm. Time, perhaps, to sample Dublin's new frontier?

Modern Irish

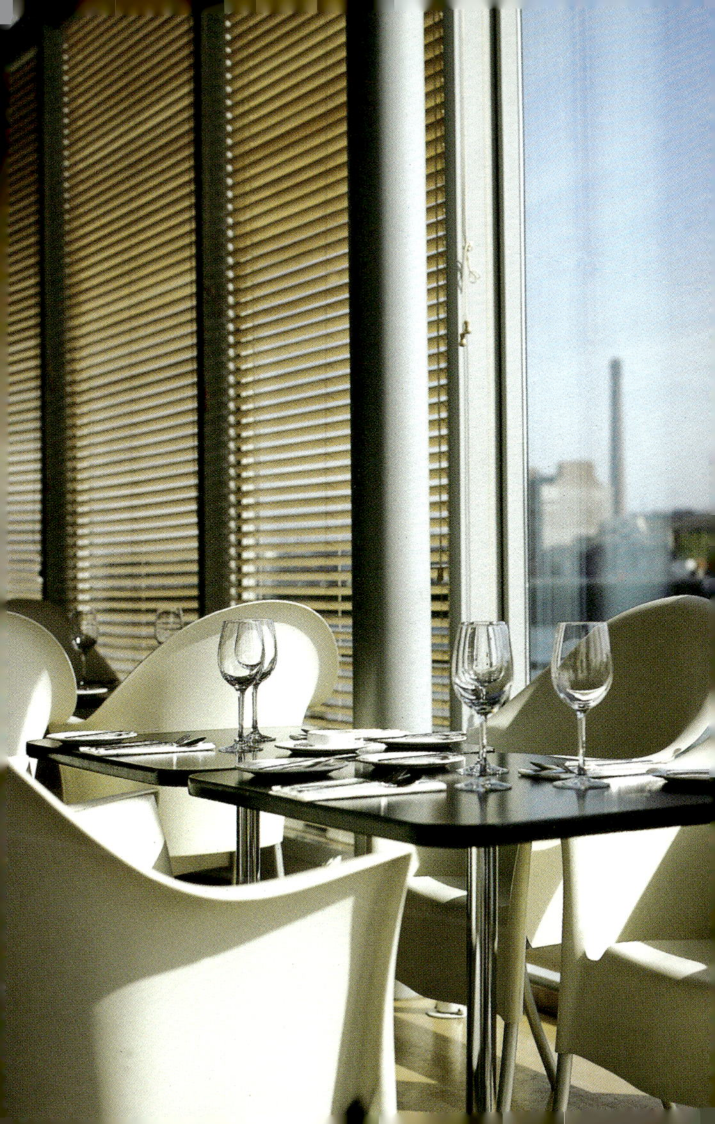

Da Roberto

5 George's Lane, Blackrock
County Dublin
t 278 0759

The first time we ate here, we thought we'd discovered the best Italian in Dublin. Next time, we could hardly get the waiter's attention to place an order. After lighting a bonfire and sending smoke signals to the kitchen, we weren't surprised that our food was burnt. And a once-unctuous buffalo mozzarella served with fabulous sheets of cured pork was now merely bland. But things had improved on our third visit. The interior is still vile (like an Italian restaurant on the Costa del Sol), but the pasta is very good, and we even met the waitress. A mushroom ravioli with creamy mushroom and bacon sauce and the spaghetti carbonara were both damn tasty. Side orders of sautéed spinach were *not*. Still, we had a quick, cheap, tasty supper. They also have a sister restaurant called Da Enzos on Richmond Road, which is considerably cheaper than Da Robertos. It's a Northside/Southside thing.

CD Italian

Dali's

63/65 Main Street, Blackrock
County Dublin
t 278 0660

Ask yourself if Ireland's reputation as a place where visitors can expect a warm welcome is worth preserving. If you think it is, don't be afraid to share that view with Irish restaurateurs. We did just this at Dali's recently, after a grumpy waitress almost ruined our meal. To be fair, the manager was very decent about it. This is a popular spot with finicky Monkstown and Blackrock ladies and it is also popular among suits with just one thing on their mind – alcohol content. In fact, Dali's is a sort of suburban Unicorn: it's comfortable, the service is excellent, the customers are drunk and the food is just okay. Try the pan fried prawns in a balsamic and lemon butter sauce, topped with crispy pancetta (€13). To follow, have the lamb, stuffed with black pudding on a bed of sage mash (€26). Now that Blueberry's has closed, this is one of only two good spots to eat in Blackrock.

Modern Irish CD

Dish

146 Upper Leeson Street
Dublin 2
t 664 2135 e info@tribeca.ie
w www.tribeca.ie

Trevor Browne says "we get lots of young barristers and media types coming in to check out the birds." He was in no mood for entertaining the likes of us when we rang to reserve a table. Trevor was furious about our review of Tribeca, which he also owns. Eventually we got a table, "but I need it back by 9.30pm." Same old story? Nope. Dinner was special – and yes, the chef knew we were coming. I had fishcakes, then lamb cutlets. Both hit the right notes. The cod main course was "all right, too fussy, the herb crust was unnecessary… it didn't lend anything to the dish." A side dish of asparagus in hollandaise sauce could easily suffice as a starter. Pannacotta pudding was wonderful, and nobody hassled us for our table at 9.30pm. We left to find our car clamped outside, so came back for brunch, and the car, the following day. Real OJ, lovely eggs Florentine and, yes, cute staff.

2 Modern Irish

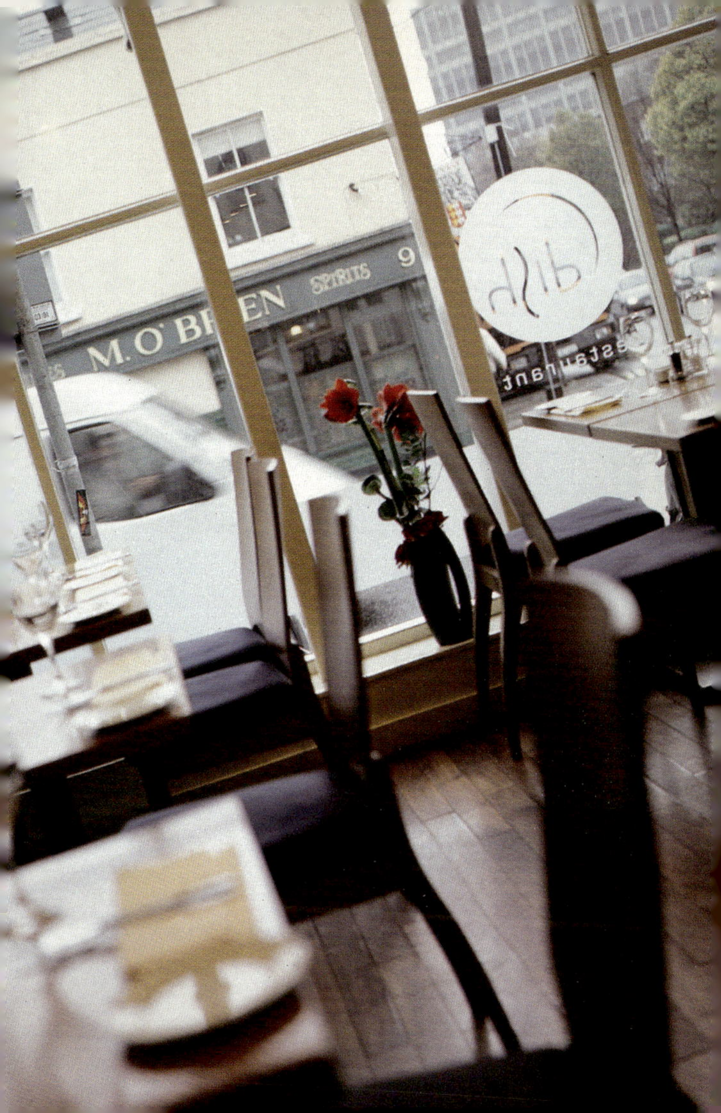
SPIRITS

Dobbins Wine Bistro

15 Stephens Lane
Dublin 2
t 661 3321 e dobbinswinebistro@eircom.net

When your table separates Charlie McCreevy from Enda Kenny, you know you're in the right place for lunch. The food has definitely taken a swing in the right direction since our last visit, but still no fireworks in the kitchen. Expensive suits with red wine teeth soak up the buzz, tossing silent bombs and chowing down on salmon, steak, prawns and spuds. All basic enough, including the sawdust-floor. But the wine list is long, like the afternoon itself. Dobbins is all about boozing, so grin and bear your liquid lunch. The staff are all shareholders, and owner John O'Byrne is a Dublin character. No wonder he's still milking it after 30 years (he set Dobbins up with Ken Bates). If you want four French boys to escort you to the loo, head up the road to Patrick Guilbaud. Dobbins is fun – but no fancy nonsense here.

2 Traditional Irish

Dunne & Crescenzi

14 & 16 South Frederick Street
Dublin 2
t 677 3815

Eileen Dunne calls it a "typical Italian *enoteca*, where you can have a glass of wine or antipasti all day." That modest description does not do justice to this honest little restaurant, where the staff are beautiful and the customers are a mixture of Trinity students with mummy and daddy, tourists and politicians (bunking off work up the road). Great bruschetta, salads and the city's best bresaola with rocket and parmesan. Cheap! Tom Doorley put D&C on the map with a glowing review in the *Tribune*. They have now had the cheek to re-draw that map by opening a string of related ventures, including a fine new branch down the road. We took Mr Doorley to lunch at the newcomer, and he couldn't tell the difference between it and the original (nothing wrong with the wine). Go, have fun and when you leave, buy some of the Italian food and drink that line the walls of this lovely homage to *la dolce vita*.

Cheap & Cheerful 2

L'Ecrivain

109a Lower Baggot Street
Dublin 2
t 661 1919 e enquiries@lecrivain.com

Yes that's PJ Mara, *schmoozing* some O'Reilly mug. Yes that's the French Ambassador, and yes that's Mrs Bono. Everyone loves this one-star Michelin debutante. Derry Clarke's food has really found its mark, stepping up to the demands of this smarter room. For example, the signature prawns in ketaifi with tartare sauce and chilli jam (€18) are not as wild and woolly as once they were. Everything is that bit neater and portions are more sensible, allowing the simplicity of a gorgeous Cos salad with Roquefort and grilled pears to shine. The venison and fillet of beef were outstanding and the chocolate dome a winner. Yes, the loos upstairs are a disgraceful after-thought, but L'Ecrivain rocks, and with a two-course lunch menu at €27 and dinner for €52, it is not expensive. By all means chuckle at poor Derry's famous claim that he makes a fiver on every €150 you spend in his restaurant. But spend it nonetheless.

2 Formal

Eden

Meeting House Square, Temple Bar
Dublin 2
t 670 5372
w www.edenrestaurant.ie

Dubliners like to play an incredibly boring game called "What's your favourite restaurant?" Rich people say Patrick Guilbaud. Gourmet snobs say Thorntons. And Domini Kemp says Chapter One. Eden used to figure somewhere too. Fashion is cruel. Tom de Paor's cool blue interior (unfairly compared to an empty swimming pool) is still cute, and there's nothing wrong with Eleanor Walsh's modern Irish cooking. Try the sirloin steak with Bearnaise sauce and chips, or the beef and Guinness stew. We adore the smokies. Uniquely for a restaurant in Temple Bar, the waiting staff are both cheerful and competent. Many of them – like manager Orla Murphy – have been here since the day it opened, which is a good sign. Finally, Sunday brunch is an institution of sorts, and particularly good fun if you are the sort of person who likes to gawk at resting actors.

Modern Irish

Elephant & Castle

18 Temple Bar
Dublin 2
t 679 3121

A mysterious New Yorker called George Schwarz owns one of the few good reasons for visiting Temple Bar – but it's usually packed, and you can't reserve. For the first time in years, we weren't asked to go away and come back at, like, midnight. After such a long delay, our expectations were high, but survived the ride. Burgers (from €8.50) were huge and juicy, accompanied by great French fries. They've cleaned up the loos ("after your grumbling in last year's guide") and the service was prompt – a little too prompt? There's still a buzz at Elephant & Castle, although it now feels middle-aged. Instead of teens and 20-somethings, we saw blue-rinse tourists and Johnny Ronan (well, he does own the building). Operating as it does on a first-come-first-served basis, I guess they're at the mercy of Temple Bar. High-point: a freshly-squeezed limeade was the real thing.

Cheap & Cheerful

Ely

22 Ely Place
Dublin 2
t 676 8986

Think Bridget Jones: short skirts, lots of make-up. The whiff of desperation. If you're a single, professional woman in your 30s, you have probably been here before. If not, make haste. If anything can save Dublin from super-pubs, it is the stylish wine bar. Wait, is that an oxymoron? Nobody thinks wine bars are stylish. Not anymore. Well, Ely is, and it may well save your private life. There are 300 types of wine. Eighty are available by the glass. The staff are lovely. The big seats downstairs are conducive to good conversation with tipsy strangers. The lighting is kind – not kind enough for some, alas – and the food is usually delicious. Try the bangers and mash, the Kilkea oysters or the beef burger – but demand chips instead of the grim potato salad. P.S. We'll get into trouble for depicting Ely as an exclusive pick-up joint. If you can't abide the thought of sex, you can always stay home alone. We're going out to play.

Modern European 2

Ernie's

Mulberry Gardens, Donnybrook
Dublin 4
t 269 3300

Older people like the calm comforts of pro staff, well-spaced tables, beautiful art and a lack of pumping music. Young bloods like to be treated like royals, without a hint of irony. So everyone goes to Ernie's. In a world of cool minimalism, it is a welcome respite. They just spent a fortune redecorating, and have even hired a PR company to spread the word, but don't get the wrong idea: this is still a gracious throwback, and why not, dammit? Last week the Caesar salad was a tad sad, but the grilled sole with lemon and parsley butter and the Dublin Bay prawns were both quite excellent. Six months ago, food was a little more average, so we hope the upward curve continues. Robert Cahill is the last of Dublin's great maitre d's. Go for the early bird menu – just €20 – make friends and linger all evening. Ernie's is that sort of place.

4 Formal

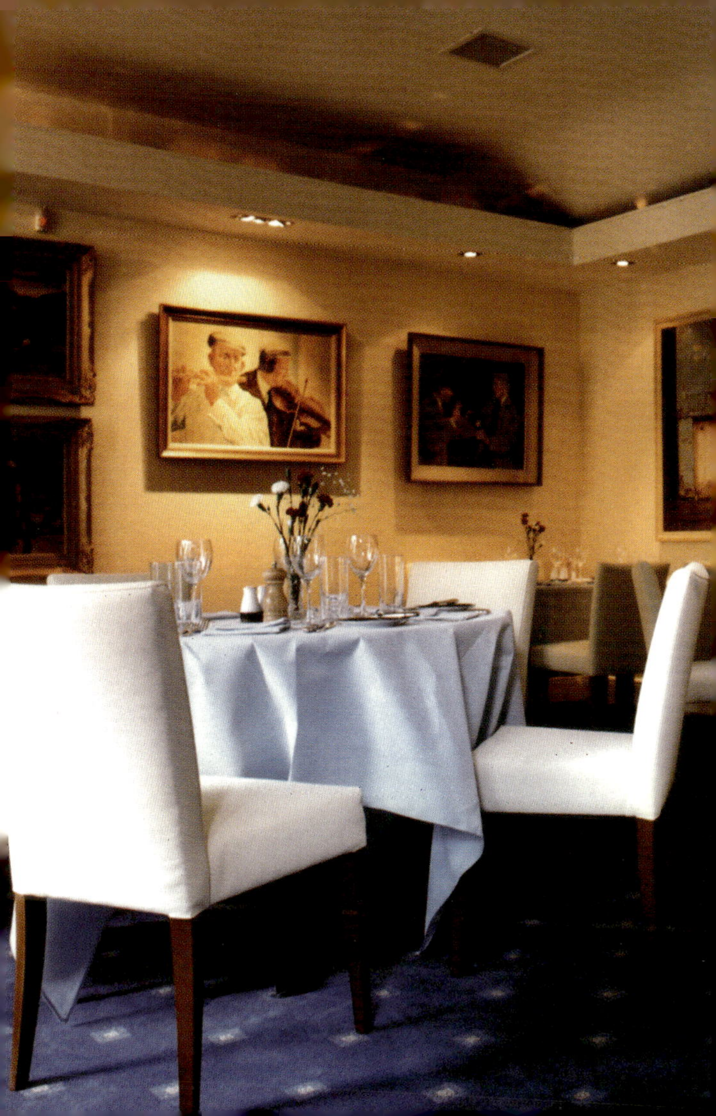

The Exchange

Westin Hotel, College Green
Dublin 2
t *645 1318*
w *www.westin.com*

This building has a colourful history, and its current owners – Johnny Ronan and Richard Barrett – are no strangers to controversy. Their tenant, the Westin Hotel, had the bad fortune to open for business on September 10, 2001. Deep pockets and strong management saw them through year one, and the hotel is beginning to feel like a part of the city at last. The basement bar does upmarket pub grub, but for better value, stay upstairs. When it's busy, the dining room feels sophisticated, elegant. When it's quiet, you're eating in a hotel. Sunday brunch is the highlight. For €35 you will get a really warm welcome, a glass of Taittinger, a rake of Sunday papers and the most lavish spread in town. Expect all the usual Irish breakfast fare, smoked salmon, oysters and a cheerful "I'll see what I can do" when mother starts getting ideas above her station.

2 Modern European

Fitzers

51 Dawson Street
Dublin 2
t *677 1155* ***e*** *eat@fitzers.ie*
w *www.fitzers.ie*

Fitzers is a chain, but the Dawson Street branch is very much the flagship. The dining room has had various incarnations over the years, at the moment it's all smooth beige and creams. There are no European waiters – manager Robert Scanlon insists on hiring only charming Antipodeans. Music is nice and some of the food was good. Also, if they have two days warning they will make the best chocolate birthday cake in the city. Lunch can work out pricey enough (there's no set menu) but there's an early bird menu in the evening, and in fairness, prices are not unreasonable. Starters are under a tenner: warm spinach and gorgonzola tart (€7.95), squid with rock salt and chilli (€9.95) were both excellent. My uncle – a pig who would eat anything – enjoyed his corn fed chicken with wild mushrooms (€19). I paid for everything. Lunch is served until 5pm, so Fitzers is also worth remembering for a late lunch date.

World 2

Four Seasons

Simmonscourt Road
Dublin 4
t 269 6446
w www.fourseasons.com

The Ice Bar is full of people who are world famous in Dublin. We prefer the other bar, which feels like a local institution after 18 months. Elsewhere in the Four Seasons, the formal dining room is one of those places where you feel obliged to sit up straight, and everything runs like clockwork. We like the café. The new menu is more diverse and hard to beat for value: we had fabulous sirloin steaks with peppercorn sauce and pommes pont neuf with Caesar salad for €25. My veal paillard with a rocket salad and chargrilled courgettes (€19.50) was delicious. Portions are generous, food is usually very good, and manager John Healy runs a fine ship. Brunch is a little too popular (always some ex you really don't want to bump into), but with two bars and a grand reception area, one can usually find a place in which to artfully slumber. Twenty-nine countries, one philosophy? Indeed.

2 Formal

Les Fréres Jacques

74 Dame Street
Dublin 2
t 679 4555

There are two good restaurants on Dame Street. If you are in The Mermaid or Les Fréres Jacques, then you have found one of them. After Guilbaud's, this is the best French restaurant in D2 – certainly in the fish department. Full of legal eagles and fat Americans, it's the sort of place where even the women wear pin-striped suits. The interior is still pokey, but they have done away with the creepy wall-paper. You will hear far too much of your neighbours' conversation, and the loos are too cramped. Last night I started with the tartine of sourdough bread with a delicate mix of cucumber and mozzarella with a little dill, roast red peppers on top with some asparagus that had been blanched and then roasted off with a little butter and balsamic. Perfect. Black sole with beurre noisette was superb – as was the lobster. The food is very good. The prices (particularly at dinner) and lack of comfort may leave you feeling sour.

Formal 2

French Paradox

53 Shelbourne Road, Ballsbridge
Dublin 4
t 660 4068
w www.fparadox.com

We love this wine shop, deli and restaurant – all lead counters, white walls, orange banquettes and stools. Have a glass of excellent grog with tasting plates of cheese, charcuterie and patés, plus salade verte or something off the foie gras menu. They do a salad Bill Hogan: good lettuce plus shavings of Desmond and Gabriel cheese drizzled with unctuous olive oil and rock salt (Ireland's answer to the Caesar salad). The upstairs restaurant is small and the wine shop is downstairs, but they will soon be cracking through to the premises next door to start selling 50 new wines and some sort of Gallic tapas. Run by Tanya (posh bird) and Pierre (Ooh-la-la), they are very charming and will help you find a decent bottle for any occasion. Space is limited, so choose your ETA carefully. Perfect place to saunter in at 3pm – stay till they throw you out seven hours later.

French

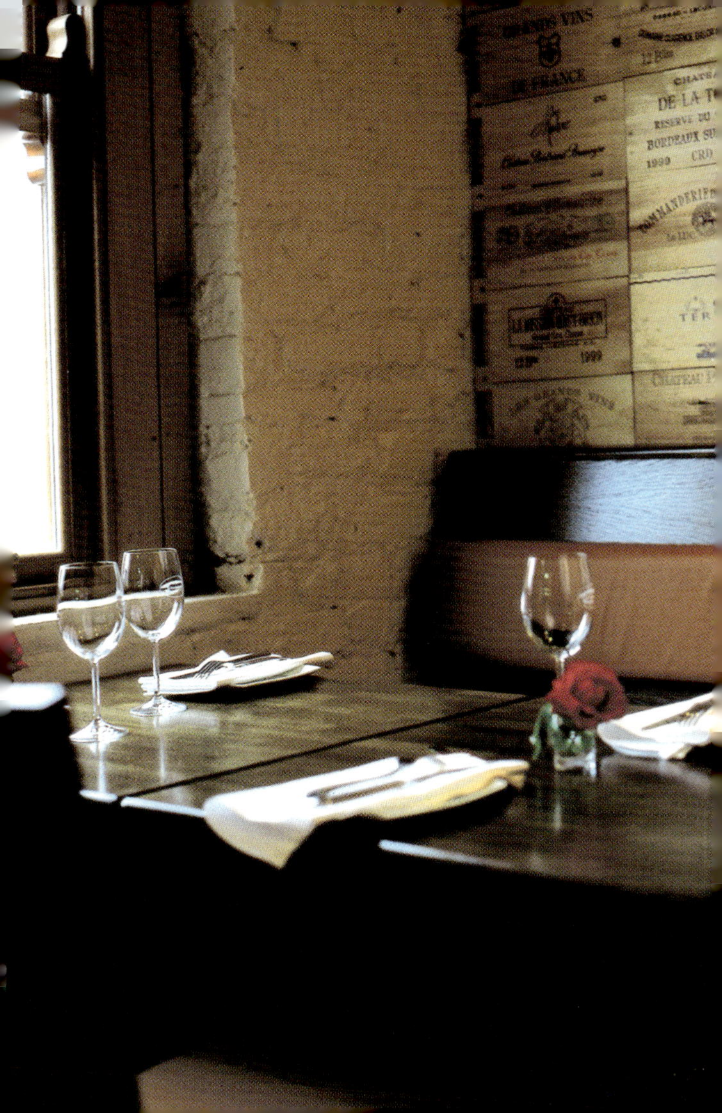
GRANDS VINS
DE FRANCE
1999

Furama

Eirpage House, Donnybrook
Dublin 4
t 283 0522

Back in the day, Gay Byrne used to have lunch here every Friday. You'll still rub shoulders with the Montrose elite. Order some Gewurtztraminer and make a pig of yourself on the crispy aromatic duck, followed by deep-fried shredded chilli beef, noodles and sizzling beef with black pepper. Finish with a cup of green tea and an empty promise to join Weight Watchers. Clean, good service and tasty grub. Very do-able pricewise – we were stuffed and wined for €50 each. But avoid Furama after the Leopardstown races: you will be accosted by red-faced, tweed-wearing, overweight horsey types singing *Patricia the Stripper*. They will ruin your banana fritters. Get revenge by reporting them to Donnybrook Garda station. Horsey types always drive drunk.

Chinese

The Gables

Foxrock Village
Dublin 18
t 289 2174

If this newcomer is still here in 2013 – alas there are no certainties in the Dublin restaurant world – it will either be a tired old lady or a local legend. Today it is a chic lunch spot for fashionable women and their irritable children who come home from London and refuse to leave the nest again. The McCabe brothers, Jim and John, have a wine shop next door – corkage is only €5. The McCabes and Anne Marie Nohl of the Expresso Bar are the people behind the Gables. Good team, great product. Light and airy, quietly sophisticated, the interior is actually beautiful, and how many restaurants can you say that about? The lunch menu is good value, particularly given the address. Avoid the chowder but demand the fish special. Scallops rock. Unisex loos. Service is fine.

Modern Irish

Govinda's

4 Aungier Street
Dublin 2
t 475 0309

If you've ever been a student, away from home in a big and slightly scary city, you have also run out of money. If you had any sense, you spent most of your time chatting up strangers and pawning your soul for dinner from strange religious sects. If you didn't get around to doing this yourself, make sure your own children do not suffer. Send them to Govinda's in New York, Prague and Beijing. Simple, clean vegetarian cafés, they are owned by the Hare Krishnas, who make great food without caffeine (makes you hyper), garlic (passionate) or mushrooms (ignorant). Pure vegetarian: no meat, fish, eggs or any of their by-products are used. The Harries are a lot less scary than the Scientologists – the manager, Nicola, knows every scandal going! – and Govinda's is great for cheap, tasty meals. Bring your mother, and if she starts moaning, tell her you're gay. That ought to shut her up.

Cheap & Cheerful

Gruel

68A Dame Street
Dublin 2
t 670 1719

Want to be pampered? You're in the wrong place. Odd tables and flimsy chairs are crowded in the back, you're expected to seat yourself and it's not unusual to see the staff preparing food on a wooden chopping block right next to your table. But Gruel isn't about the space; it's about the food, which is good and cheap. Hearty, fresh-baked rolls are made in-house. Daily sandwich specials (€5.75) range from delicious roast lamb with apricot chutney, to turkey with cranberry sauce and stuffing. The pizza (€3.50 per slice) is also great. Soup is served in gigantic bowls with more of that delicious bread, and there are home-made desserts like brownies and banana cake. Weekend brunch is a must. Have French toast with maple syrup and strips of bacon (€7.80). The people behind the Mermaid – which is next door – have, in Gruel, mastered the art of simple food, made well and sold cheap. A winner.

Cheap & Cheerful

Halo at The Morrison

Ormand Quay, Dublin 1
t 878 2999 e halo@morrisonhotel.ie
w www.morrisonhotel.ie

Lunch-times here are rarely busy. Maybe one buffalo and one Indian dot the vast prairie. I started with a tartare of salmon, wasabi crème fraîche, dill and cucumber salad. Wasabi is the ferocious Japanese horse-radish which usually makes your sinuses feel raped by a Dyna-rod. This wasabi was exquisite. The tarte of smoked haddock, leeks, crème fraiche and rocket salad was a warm, old-fashioned treat. A casserole of guinea hen, root vegetables and truffle cream was comfort eating carried to Elysian heights. My pan-fried fillet of beef was a massive lump, tender as butter and utterly delicious. Lunch is €25 for two courses, €29 for three, and they don't serve elegant wisps of food. Elsewhere in the Morrison – still up for sale – the bar is all big leather couches, and downstairs, DJ Martin Thomas gets girls to shake their tails. All quite cosmo, for such a dirty town.

1 French

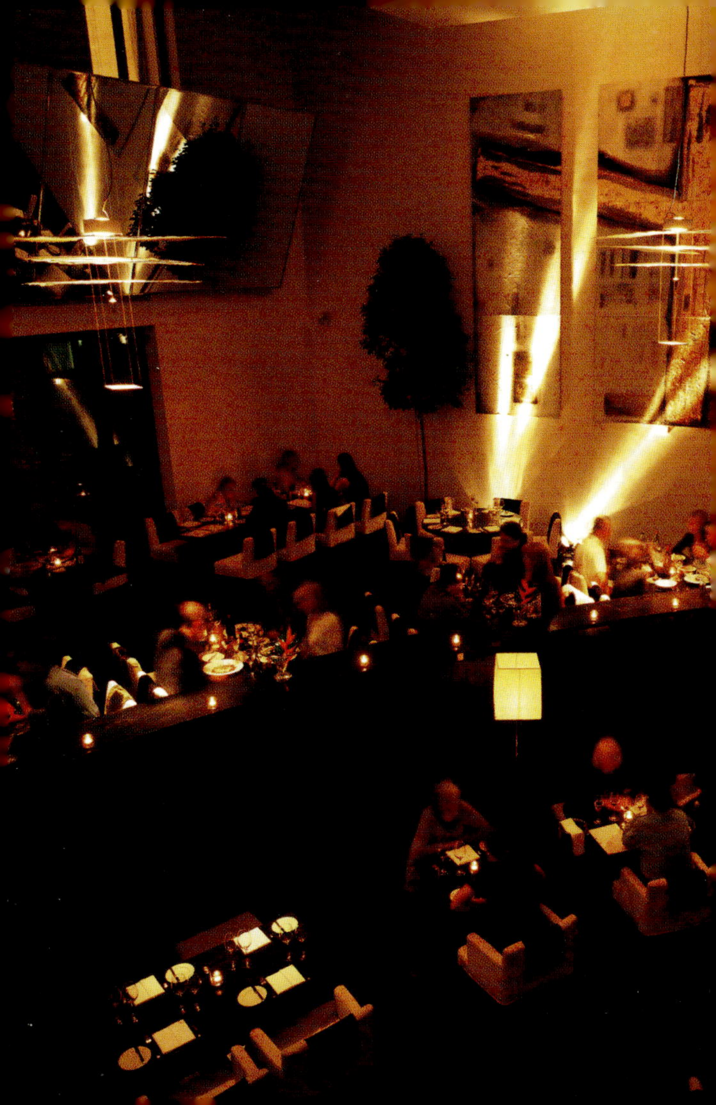

Hanley at the Bar

The Distillery Building, May Lane
Dublin 7
t 878 0104

Smithfield is a good example of what happens when some genius in central planning decides to make a place "trendy." Instead of celebrating one truly cultural event, the Smithfield Horse Fair, said genius tried to get rid of it. Then he – it could only be a man – installed some crap ethnic restaurants and yuppies who think they're artists; hence those studio apartments. It's enough to make one yearn for Ballymun, the last real vestige of culture in Dublin (yes, we know that's going too). To be fair, Smithfield is home to the Dice Bar, as close as Dublin gets to Nolita. So it's not all bad. Claire Hanley's restaurant only serves lunch. All those lawyers and judges make it an ideal place for a game of Spot The Unholy Alliance. None of the mains cost more than €11.50, and you can stick to an open sandwich and soup (€10) if you want. The décor is slick and service is okay. Call it a handsome refuge.

7 Modern Irish

Havana

3 Camden Market, Grantham Street
Dublin 8
t 476 0046 e info@havana.ie

We used to love Havana. You walk into this small tapas bar and immediately sense that there's fun to be had. The interior is pretty and the 30-something customers are prettier still. You get the distinct impression that the Irish aren't so ugly after all. But the last time we ate here, the waiter was hopelessly over-worked and the food was mediocre. What a shame, because the owners are obviously conscientious – they send an email out to regular customers, announcing new successes – and one of us lives around the corner. If you must eat, try the paella (€6.95) and the marinated tiger prawns with salsa rosa (€7.25). Still, at least it's not expensive. Post-script: our Art Director has taken grave exception to this review. She insists that punters have a lot of fun in Havana, the music is great, the food is okay and it's cheap. She is not a woman to offer praise lightly, so we feel obliged to record her remarks.

Spanish 8

Jaipur

5 St James Terrace, Malahide
County Dublin
t 8455 455 e info@jaipur.ie
w www.jaipur.ie

Dublin has a plague of generic curry houses; we are fast becoming a carbon copy of a provincial English town. Bad Indian food is basically the worst thing in the world, apart from Westlife. Good Indian food is rare and exquisite. In all three branches of Jaipur – Dalkey, town and now Malahide – the interior is spacious, the service is magnificent and the food is exquisite. Try the meen var curry (€17), full of something called butterfish (it's a plump, white fish, somewhere between cod and monkfish). The rogan josh is aromatic and tasty while side orders of beans poriyal (green beans with lentils, €4.75) and ad tarka palak (not otter, as someone suggested, but spinach with garlic and butter, €4.75) were splendid. Paddy Power boss Stewart Kenny and Riverdeep Chairman Pat McDonagh are regulars. Finally, our favourite Maitre D', Nisheeth Tak, has returned to Jaipur after a short stint in Vermillion.

CD Indian

Kilkenny Centre Café

6 Nassau Street, Dublin 2
t 677 7066

Billy Connolly says the traffic on Nassau Street respects neither lights nor people – "I almost lost my toes" he moaned, last time he was in town. The Big Yin likes homemade scones and lashings of tea in this first floor den for country grannies. They trade long tales about wayward children. Does this popular talking-shop really have – as they claim – the best view in Dublin? No. In truth you'll see a stuttering line of buses delivering the next batch of German tourists into the welcoming arms of Dublin gurriers. But the food is, at least, consistent. The seafood chowder (€4.45) is wholesome and delicious and you will get a fine breakfast here too. Hot lunch specials (€10.95) vary daily. Avoid the sweet and sour chicken – all too like a tired school dinner – and stick to Oirish staples like the beef and Guinness casserole with basil mash and baby carrots.

Cheap & Cheerful 2

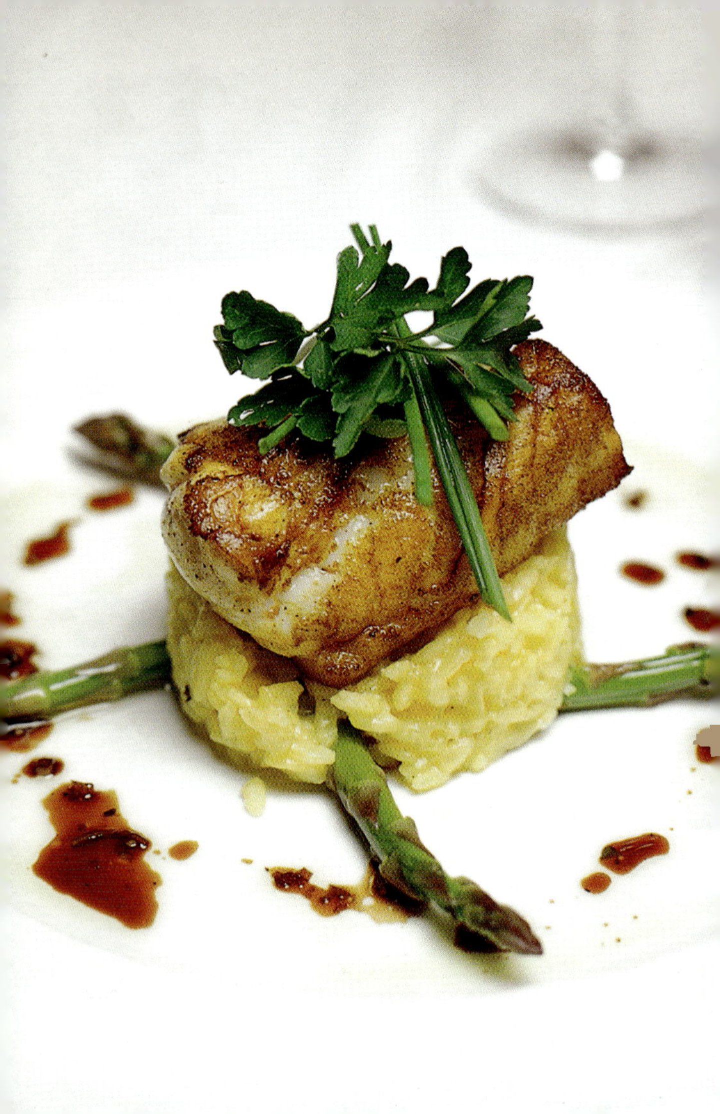

Kevin Arundel at Number Ten

Longfields Hotel, 10 Lower Fitzwillian Street
Dublin 2
t 676 1060 e info@longfields.ie
w www.longfields.ie

Some of our moans and groans have been addressed. Tableware is smart, service is sharper and Kevin Arundel's food is still good value and tasty (he used to work at the wonderful Marlfield House). Three-course lunch will set you back €28, which is – let's face it – no longer expensive. Seared scallops with asparagus and black lard were licked off the plate. Tasty leek and potato soup appeased man-friend. Corn-fed chick with casserole of veg and Madeira jus was delicious, and Kevin's signature dish – hot oysters with mango and curry sabayon – is always wonderful. A new bar was being constructed as we munched, and profits from brunch down at the Schoolhouse will fund gradual tweaks to the dining room here. Looking around, it's clearly a place for savvy girls and boys to do lunch.

Modern European 2

Kinara

318 Clontarf Road
Dublin 3
t 833 6759
w www.kinara.ie

The Christian right is neither. We prefer Eastern religions, which are all about serenity. Alas, most Eastern restaurants are garish. Overlooking the gentle calm of Bull Island, you will find no flock-horror tactics at Kinara – just crisp furnishings and subtle layers of light. The food is equally confident and understated. Start with chanp kandhari (charcoal cooked lamb chops marinated in garlic, tumeric and chilli, €8.80), delicately cooked yet generously presented. Follow with parsi jhinga (sweet and sour tiger prawns with tamarind, red chilli and coriander, €19.10) or the Bengalese machali achari (red snapper simmered in pickles, curry leaves and vinegar, €14.95). Even that traditional stumbling block – dessert – was exceptional: a homemade pistachio ice cream. Clontarf, your secret is out. Go, eat, worship.

Indian

TAKE A FRESH LOOK.

The Dubliner

The King Sitric

East Pier, Howth
County Dublin
t832 5235 e info@kingsitric.ie
w www.kingsitric.ie

Joan and Aidan MacManus have now renovated their 32-year-old restaurant and rooms overlooking Howth harbour. The location is still delightful – walk that pier before dinner. You'll be welcomed in the new bar area, shown to your table, offered drinks and issued with a cheerful invitation to poke around the temperature-controlled wine cellar, with its vast selection of classic French wines. For starters try the buttermilk crab bake (€12.70), or the grilled scallops with black and white pudding (€10.80). If you are trying to impress, share lobster cooked three ways – steamed, grilled and served in 'Dublin Lawyer' sauce – for €108. Service was clumsy the last time we ate here, and many of the fish dishes seemed, well, tired. We are not suggesting that they go all fusion on us, but the food does need to lighten up – in other words, get rid of the heavy white wine sauces.

CD Seafood

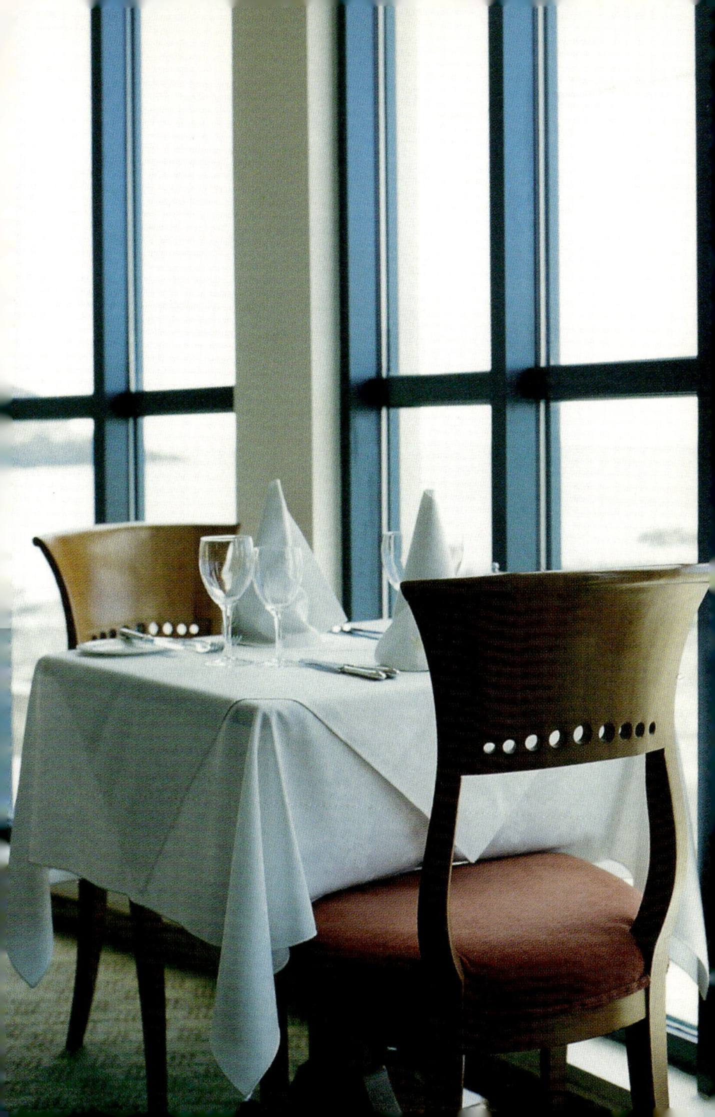

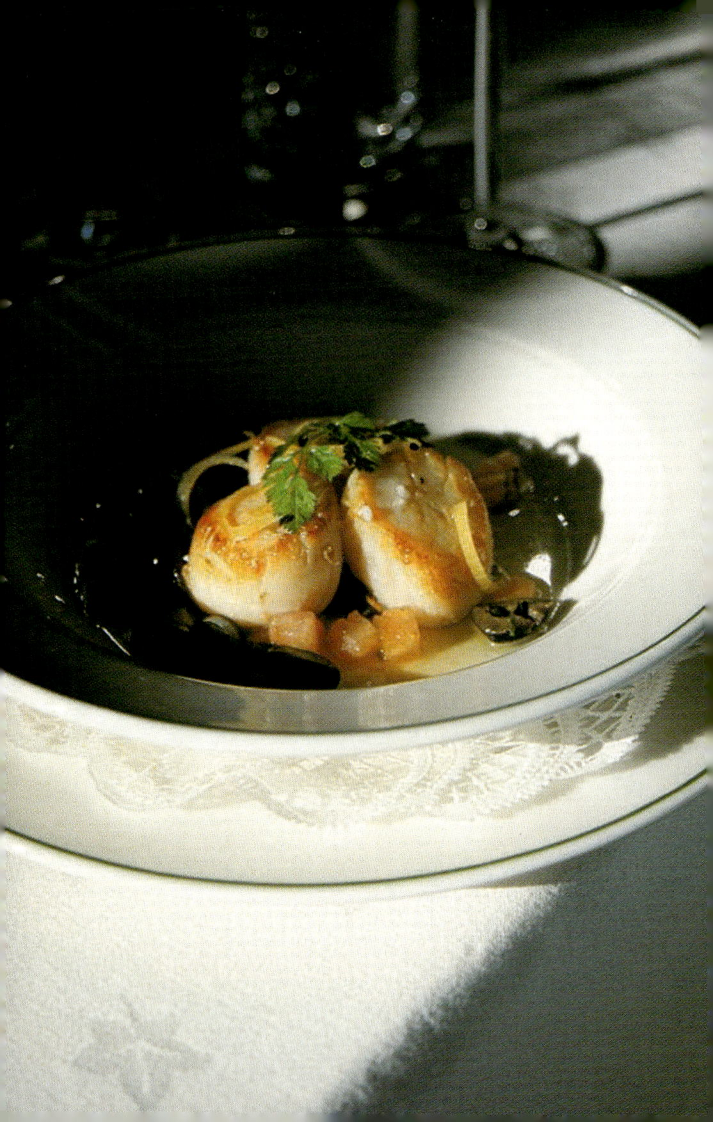

Kish

Coliemore Road, Dalkey
County Dublin
t 2850377
w www.kishrestaurant.ie

When Kish opened, we thought it was great. Things went pear-shaped (they lost their chef and sommelier) and service suffered. A new chef, Roisin Gavin (who used to work at Dean's in Belfast) is bringing new life to this seaside stunner. Gawk at porpoises, seals and diving cormorants from your window seat. Sunday lunch here is excellent – but at €40 a head it demands a special occasion. Squab with pasta and black pudding sounded frightening, but was rich and delicious, as was the cured salmon with Niçoise garnish. Cod with peas and sautéed cabbage was tasty. Fish was a little over-cooked for our liking, but then again, Sunday lunch clientele probably don't go for nouvelle cuisine. The chocolate tart and the citrus crème brulée were two-star in quality, as were the petits fours. Good to see this dame back on her feet – as long as the food stays consistent and the service remains sweet, Kish is worth re-discovering.

Seafood CD

Locks

1 Windsor Terrace, Portobello
Dublin 8
t 454 3391

Can Locks remain a player? We hope so – but starters close to €20 and mains twice that should be pretty fantastic. The location is adorable and the older waiting staff are still charming. Head waiter Liam has been here for 17 years, and his team earn their hefty 12.5% service charge. The menu is full of the same old favourites – but are they? The signature starter of potato skins with spinach, prawns, smoked salmon and hollandaise was on a plate so hot, the hollandaise had split (left too long under the salamander) and the spinach was tough and stalky. The asparagus starter was pleasant, served with some olive oil dressing or hollandaise with a little Parma ham – too plain to justify the price of €17.40. The monkfish was just okay. The wine list is good, and there is a set lunch menu for €28.95, but Locks feels ever so slightly shabby. P.S. As we go to press, a new chef arrives. Typical!

8 Formal

La Maison des Gourmets

15 Castle Market
Dublin 2
t 672 7258

Penny Plunkett worked for Patrick Guilbaud for ten years. The Michelin maestro has shares in Penny's bakery and a café that is better than most of Dublin's restaurants. The menu breathes confidence and experience – it is small but perfectly formed. You can have great soup, salad, savoury tartes and tartines (that's posh sandwiches to you) for lunch. All put together with genuine Gallic flair. Hot French onion soup is a take-away snip at €3. After a lean period downstairs (fire destroyed their bakery in the Liffey Trust centre), the buttery croissants, tartes aux fruits and crusty bread are also available to go; if you have to bring dessert to a dinner party, your hostess will clap hands with delight at the sight of a Maison des Gourmets box. Upstairs again, afternoon tea is becoming something of an institution – great coffee, wonderful pastries and sun pouring in the window.

French 2

Mao

2/3 Chatham Row
Dublin 2
t 670 4899 e info@cafemao.com

We can never understand why lefties didn't get irate when Graham and Rosie Campbell opened a restaurant called Mao. Did they not think it odd that the memory of a murderous dictator – a man, remember, who starved his own people – should be used to flog Asian food? Or did they appreciate the irony? We think the name is tasteless, but have really got to loosen up. The cooking is fine – upmarket Asian fast food. Stick to staples like chilli squid, Thai fishcakes or Nasi Goreng. Chilli-phobes, dieters and kiddies are all well looked after. Table turnover is high, and the staff all seem to get on, so it usually has a vibrant atmosphere. On a sunny day, grab a table outside, swig a bottle of Tiger beer and pretend that Dublin has always been so chilled.

Thai

La Mère Zou

22 St Stephens Green
Dublin 2
t 661 6669

A very sweet basement bistro, perfect for singletons, tourists or rosemantic couples looking to taste a bit of France. The "big plates" at lunch are great – a combo small starter and main course all on one plate. Try La Landaise: a little smoked duck salad on one edge of the plate, some confit duck and sautéed spuds on the other. Supper is all bistro grub – goats' cheese salads, poached eggs with bacon and mushrooms, mussels (served with a million different garnishes) followed by ribs of beef (*pour deux*). Dessert – chocolate torte – was sticky, heavy and delicious and the wine list had lots of good bottles that one doesn't often see. Service is usually charming, despite the kitchen's occasional dips, and the location couldn't be better.

French 2

The Mermaid

69/70 Dame Street
Dublin 2
t 670 8236
w www.mermaid.ie

There are too many tables. The seats are desperately uncomfortable. But everyone loves the Mermaid Café. Ronan Ryan is a fine manager and head chef Temple Garner – another refugee from Il Primo – is equally ambitious. We love brunch on a Saturday. If drink has the better of you, try the rib-eye steak with home fries and fried eggs (plus a dash of béarnaise to ensure cardiac problems) or the smoked cod with horseradish mash and sautéed spinach. Fabulous salads (thank-you Lord) and an unusual wine-list also appeal to regulars like John Banville and Louis le Brocquy. Note: the idea that the Mermaid is all New England and Atlantic grub with hints of Dame Street is nonsense. It's a mid-priced restaurant serving good and sometimes brilliant fodder, with plummy wines and casual service. Incidentally, they also have a private dining room; scene of many a *Dubliner* session.

Milano

38 Dawson Street
Dublin 2
t *670 7744*
w *www.pizzaexpress.com*

Eleven million people have AIDS in sub-Saharan Africa. By 2010, there will be 20 million victims. Pondering these figures will not put you in the mood for *haute cuisine*. Hence Milano. Full of beautiful poor people, this stylish branch of Pizza Express (there's another one in Temple Bar) is typical of an English chain. Find a formula, make it work and let it run – in this case, all the way to Galway. The thin-crust pizza is always okay – it comes out of a pre-packed pile. Stick to trademark combinations like Fiorentina (€9.95) with spinach, egg, olives, garlic or the Veneziana (capers, pine kernels, mozzarella and tomatoes, €7.95). Or make up your own combination if nothing takes your fancy – but no pineapple, please. The wine list is a little sparse, with too many grotty Italians for our liking. But how wrong can you go with pizza?

Italian 2

Monty's of Kathmandu

28 Eustace Street, Temple Bar
Dublin 2
t 670 4911
w www.montys.ie

Woody Harrelson says it's "the best restaurant in the world," which proves how potent Irish pot really is. Monty's is the only Nepalese kitchen in the country, and one of our favourite ethnic restaurants. The modern, cream interior is a bit poky – threaten to leave if they ask to sit you in the basement – but at least it eschews the Bollywood production values of mainstream Asian joints. Relaxed, friendly staff describe dishes with passion, and with good reason. Mick Lally and Jim Corr love the famous Momo dumplings (€14), but remember to order them 24 hours before you arrive. Otherwise, try the poleko squid (€8) or Monty's other signature dish, kachala (€12.95), raw minced lamb with herbs, spices and a shot of whiskey. It's a delicacy among the Newars in Kathmandu and typical of dear old Monty: never greasy, always spicy, without being hot-hot-hot.

Nepalese

Nosh

111 Coliemore Road, Dalkey
County Dublin
t 284 0666
w www.nosh.ie

There are many reasons why restaurants do not survive. Chief among them is hazy goodwill. Don't open a restaurant unless you know exactly how much business you need to do – and *can* do. With that in mind, we're not sure how Samantha and Sacha Farrell make any money with such a small dining room. Mind you, this Dalkey delight is usually packed out from lunch through dinner, all day, every day. As you would expect from two ex-Expresso Bar girls, the interior is smart, bright and stylish. Signature dishes include fish & chips with sumo fat fries and tartare sauce (€16.50) and the seared Thai beef salad with noodles and soya lime (€8.75). We recommend weekend brunch: read the papers, tuck into a cheese steak sambo and then walk off all those calories with a lovely stroll down to Coliemore harbour. Someone should remove Dalkey's head from its bum, though we do think it's rather cute.

Modern European CD

O'Connells

Bewley's Hotel, Merrion Road
Dublin 4
t 647 3304 e info@oconnellsballsbridge.com
w www.oconnellsballsbridge.com

It's easy to forget about O'Connells as the Four Seasons has taken over Ballsbridge. When you want to sit out on a rare sunny day this is a good place to keep in mind, especially as the wine list is pleasant and reasonable, and they do a dinner menu for just €25. Try the French onion soup or the smoked salmon, and follow with roast pork, grilled rib-eye or fish and chips. They do a wonderful tasting plate of desserts. Dinners are all mammy-style with loads of roast potatoes, sautéed carrots and roast turnips. Irish producers are given lots of mention on the menu, and yes, owner Tom O'Connell is Darina Allen's brother. Lunchtime is a bit more humbling – think carvery madness in D4. Somehow, it doesn't have the same appeal. Still, the service has settled down, and they seem to have found their niche in life. Child-friendly too.

4 Modern Irish

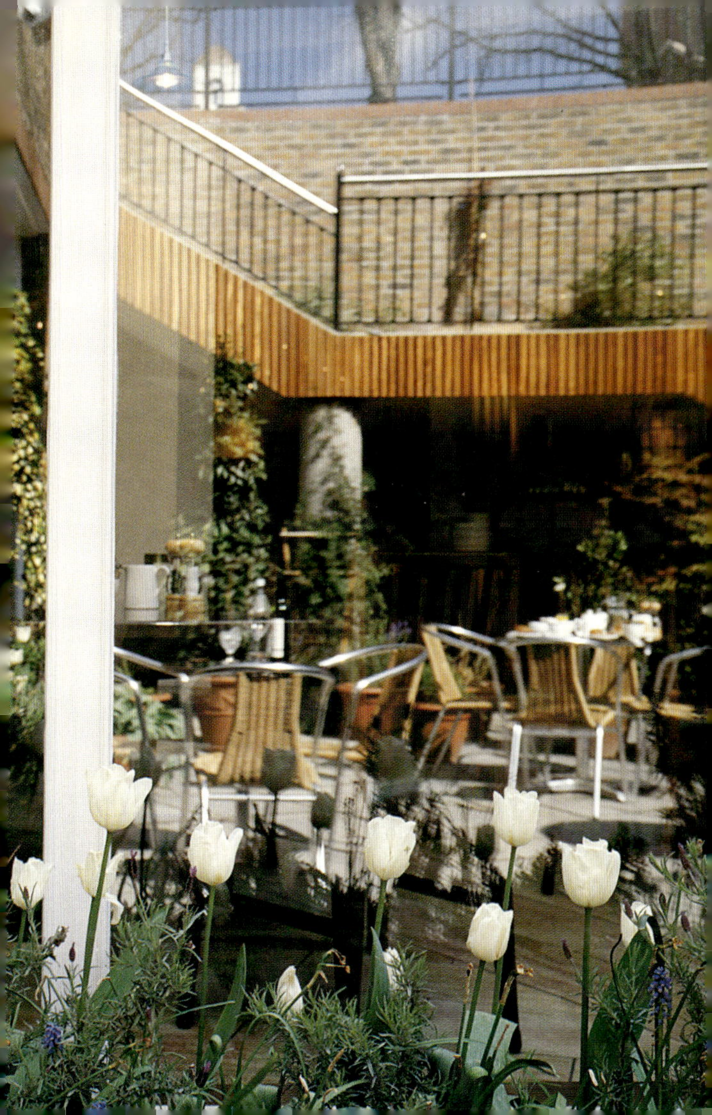

Ocean

Charlotte Quay Dock
Dublin 4
t 668 8862

Our friend Grellan said someone had given him a boat. "Sure," we said, and laughed. "No really, it cost me nothing." So we went down to Charlotte Quay, had a pint in Ocean and continued along the dock. Sure enough, the boat was there, and sinking. "I've just got to get it up." He's not alone. Back to Ocean for consolation pints ("One day you'll sail that boat"). Looking out over this watery patch of Dublin reborn, one forgives romantic thoughts. Dreams are okay. Alas the food will wake you up. In a setting like this, one needs fine fare to fuel the fantasy that Dublin is quite this chic. Alas the food is bland – aggressively bland! – and liberties are taken with that term "casual dining." Stick to seafood chowder, the scallops or a steak. Avoid the beef enchiladas (€9.95). Brunch is good. Allegedly.

The Old Schoolhouse

*Coolbanagher Church Road, Swords
County Dublin
t 840 2846
w www.oldschoolhouse.ie*

There are few good restaurants on the Northside – that's not snobbery. Blame history and geography. Still, if you're picking someone up from the airport, you live locally or you feel like a long drive, check out this 1832 schoolhouse. You can almost hear the crack of cane on bum, and when you read the specials on the period blackboard, you will probably curse Peig Sayers. Fair play to Brian and Anne Sinclair for creating a comfortable restaurant out of such an austere building. Head chef Paul Lewis does "contemporary Irish cuisine with French influences." Stick to fish specials, like Dublin Bay prawns with a simple green salad (€19) or the seared scallops with black pudding (€26). There's a small patio outside, which is nice for drinks on a summer evening, and the Kiwi manageress is an absolute darling. Beware: they want planning permission for an extension and, you guessed it, pub licence. From schoolhouse to bar... all *very* Irish.

Modern European CD

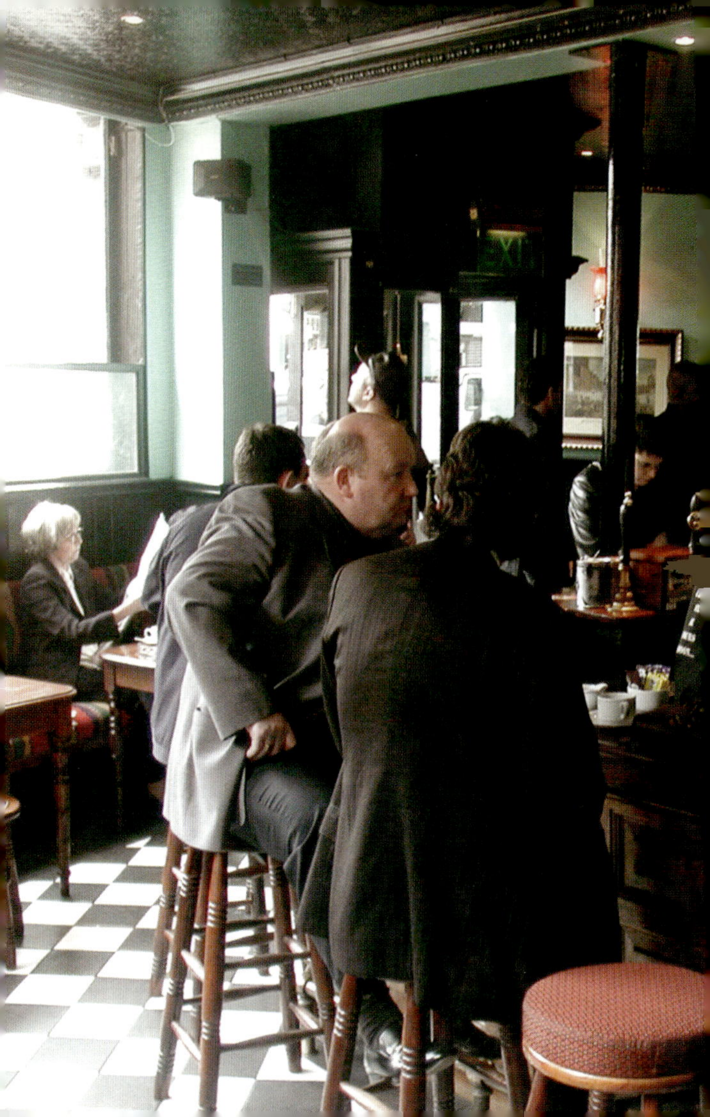

The Old Stand

37 Exchequer Street
Dublin 2
t 677 7220

Most publicans regard bar food as a nuisance rather than an integral part of the good pub experience. But Davy Byrne's is different. Redmond Doran's family have owned and managed this art deco gem for three generations. His brothers Colclough and Michel run the Old Stand, which is also just off Grafton Street. Both pubs merit inclusion here, but our office is beside the latter, so we are biased. Basically the Old Stand is comfortable, clean and welcoming. The Guinness is superb. The food is good enough to share with posh clients, your parents and visitors in search of the real Dublin. Try the homemade meatball with sautéed onions and chips, or else have the plaice. Tourists love the Irish stew, and you can see why: that respect for tradition is evident throughout. So you're not surprised when the bar-man tells you that Michael Collins had his State offices next door. It's an Old Stand thing to say.

Traditional Irish

The Olive Tree

Islamic Cultural Centre, 19 Roebuck Road
Clonskeagh
Dublin 14
t 208 0000

What can you do to save the world? You could start, I suppose, by begging George Bush to resign. If you want to do something more practical, go to the Islam Centre in Clonskeagh, and have lunch in the Olive Tree – which is really just a nice canteen. We started with tabouleh, stuffed vine leaves and various bean salads with some tzatziki-type dressing. Two chefs stood behind the counter, heaping piles of rice onto large plates and topping them with chicken Korma, chicken schwarma or chicken curry, lamb curry, meat balls and some other dish that looked like a chicken lasagne. We tried a bit of everything: all decent quality, all well seasoned. The garlic sauce that came with the pitta bread and grilled chicken pieces was particularly good. We finished with two sweet pastries, one like baklava and the other with almond. Very cheap, very good, but no booze. Go on, do your bit.

World

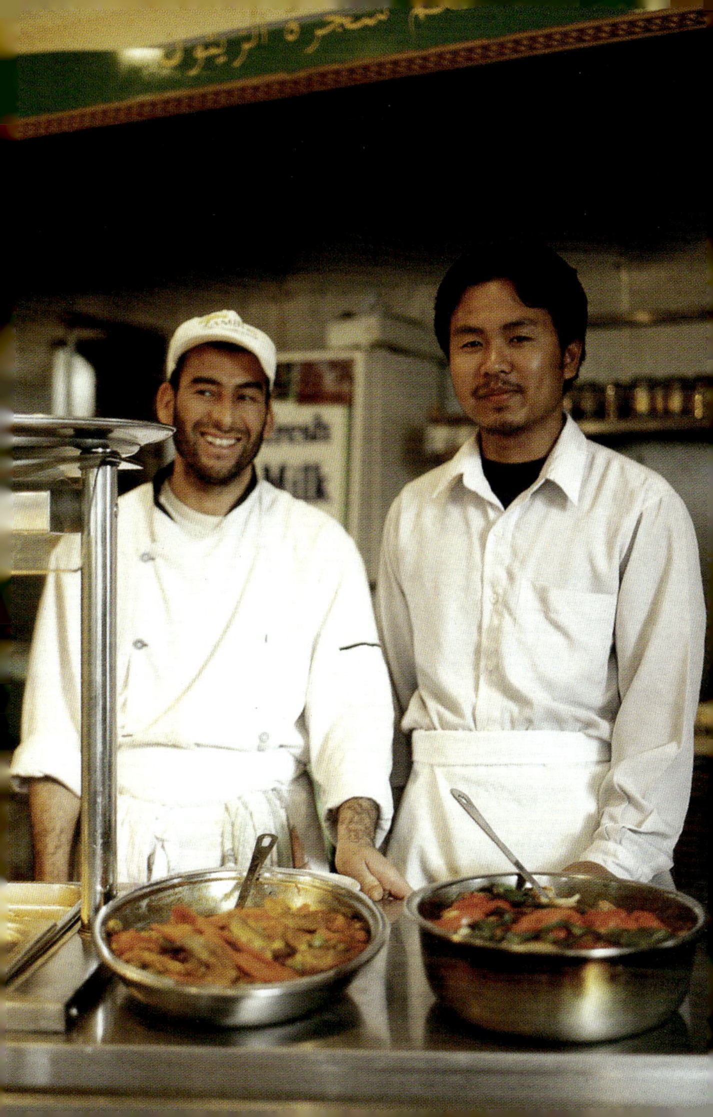

One Pico

5/6 Molesworth Place
Schoolhouse Lane, off Stephens Green
Dublin 2
t *676 0300*
w *www.onepico.com*

We had a rotten experience, soon after One Pico moved to its new home. But other critics love Eamon O'Reilly – the *Irish Times* called him the new Conrad Gallagher, which is supposed to be a compliment. It's a bit like calling Colin Farrell the new Oliver Reed. To be fair, O'Reilly's cooking is more colourful than his social life. Despite closing Pacific and opening Bleu Bistro in a matter of weeks, the chef seems determined to stay the course. In premises once occupied by the glamorous Polo One – where socialites and errant secretaries had long, boozy lunches – you will find posh grub at reasonable prices. Food is mature, confident. Try the scallops and black pudding with crushed artichokes. Fillet of veal, served with sautéed ceps mash, baby spinach and truffle cream is truly excellent (€24.76), as is the fillet of beef (€24.06). Staff are efficient, although others have moaned about eccentric service.

2 Formal

The Osborne

Portmarnock Hotel and Golf Links
Strand Road
County Dublin
t 846 0611
w www.portmarnock.com

From one tycoon's lair to another: chef Mark Doe worked in the Merrion Hotel before Tony O'Reilly poached him for his personal Northside fiefdom. That's not quite true; Sir Anthony "has no hand in the day-to-day running of..." But then, he never does, right? The Portmarnock Hotel is one of those grand monuments of Ireland reborn, all fancy oils and ghastly lighting. There's no set-price menu in the restaurant, which pretty much says it all. Never mind the prices, feel the quality; that's what you're supposed to think anyway. It's called the Osborne Restaurant because Walter Osborne painted "in the area." The food is not so tacky. Stick to the seafood – fresh from Howth – at this fancy 80-seater. Best dish? Fillet of sea bass with grilled scallops and celeriac (€28.90). Booking essential: it's only open for dinner, and closed on Sundays and Mondays.

Formal CD

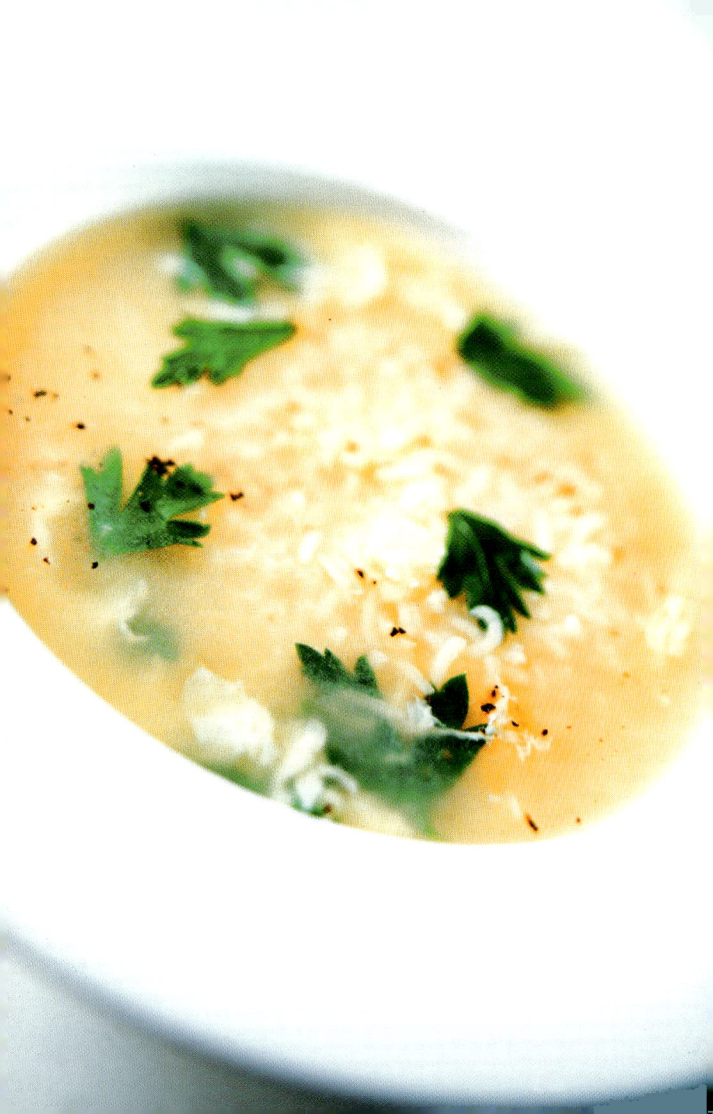

Papaya

8 Ely Place
Dublin 2
t 676 0044
w www.papaya.ie

This place used to be Snipes, a cavernous wine bar that closed down and – surprise, surprise – it's now a Thai restaurant. Useful for surreptitious outings, or evenings when you want cheap, cheerful and easy on the palate. Clear soups, prawn wontons and chicken satay are all under €8, while beef salads, curries and noodle dishes are a bit more expensive. Service was a bit one-man-bandish. No doubt, nieces and nephews would be summoned into service if they were jammers. Clean, pleasant and friendly. To be honest, there is very little that distinguishes the Thai restaurants featured in this book. Differences are usually cosmetic – interiors, ornate staff uniforms and location. Still, Papaya is a good one to remember, particularly when the Ely Wine Bar is full.

Thai 2

Patrick Guilbaud

*The Merrion Hotel, 21 Upper Merrion Street
Dublin 2*
t 676 4192
e restaurantpatrickguilbaud@eircom.net

The most famous Frenchman in Ireland plays a lot of golf, and his other interests – such as La Maison des Gourmets – must occupy some of his time. Does Restaurant Patrick Guilbaud suffer? Nope. The city's most hallowed dining room continues to dazzle in all the right places – sublime service, a surprisingly cheap lunch menu – and it seems as if Patrick is always there, shaking hands and smiling at blondes in the manner of a slightly smug child who has just inherited a large family concern. When Patrick is not around, Stefan Robin runs this tycoon's café with easy grace (shame about those awful uniforms). Head chef Guillaume Le Brun has made two-star Michelin history, with a hint of Celtic indulgence – like side orders of unctuous spuds at lunchtime. All three men have every right to be proud of this aging stunner. Don't even begin to take your opinion of Dublin restaurants seriously until you have dined at the best.

French

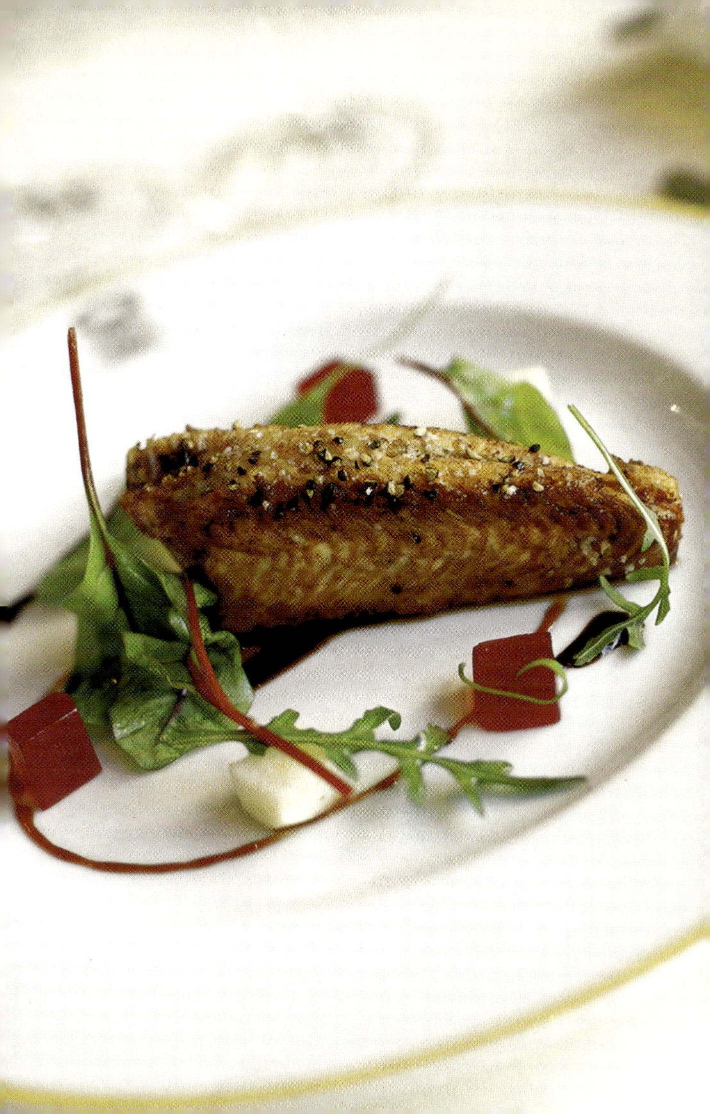

PD's Woodhouse

1 Coliemore Road, Dalkey
County Dublin
t 284 9399

Now ten years old, PD's Woodhouse is one of those neighbourhood restaurants that could only survive in a place like Santa Monica, Martha's Vineyard… or Dalkey. It looks cheap, and of course it's *not*. It looks informal, laid-back, and then you meet your boss with his mistress. What makes the Woodhouse different from every other restaurant in Dublin? "We grill on oak wood out front, not gas." So what? It's probably still carcinogenic. Staples like the huge Surf n' Turf (€28.50) with heart-cloggingly decadent dips or the sirloin steak and baked potatoes (€27) are delicious. The service is very good. Owners Peter White and Helen Argyle are engaging hosts. Besides, this being Dalkey, you will probably sit beside – which here means 'on top of' – a celebrity. Listening to their inane prattle will somehow seem rather important.

CD World

Il Posto

10 St Stephen's Green
Dublin 2
t 679 4769

We always want to like this place. Proprietor Amanda Jackson is charming. But Il Posto is in a basement, it's not particularly comfortable and when it's busy you have to scream to be heard. At least it's not as expensive as some of the rip-off Italian joints elsewhere in the city. And the food feels vaguely authentic, which makes it almost unique. Chef Sean Drugan worked at Daphne's and The Collection in London. Start with polpette de Carnevale, Italian sausage and beef meatballs in breadcrumbs with a sweet chilli and basil tomato dressing (€9). Follow it with the pan-fried calves liver with braised balsamic green lentils and roast pepperoni. We weren't wild about the pasta – but admired the quantity. So there you go: the location is splendid, prices are reasonable and portions are generous. Remember Miss Piggy's advice: "never eat more than you can lift."

Italian 2

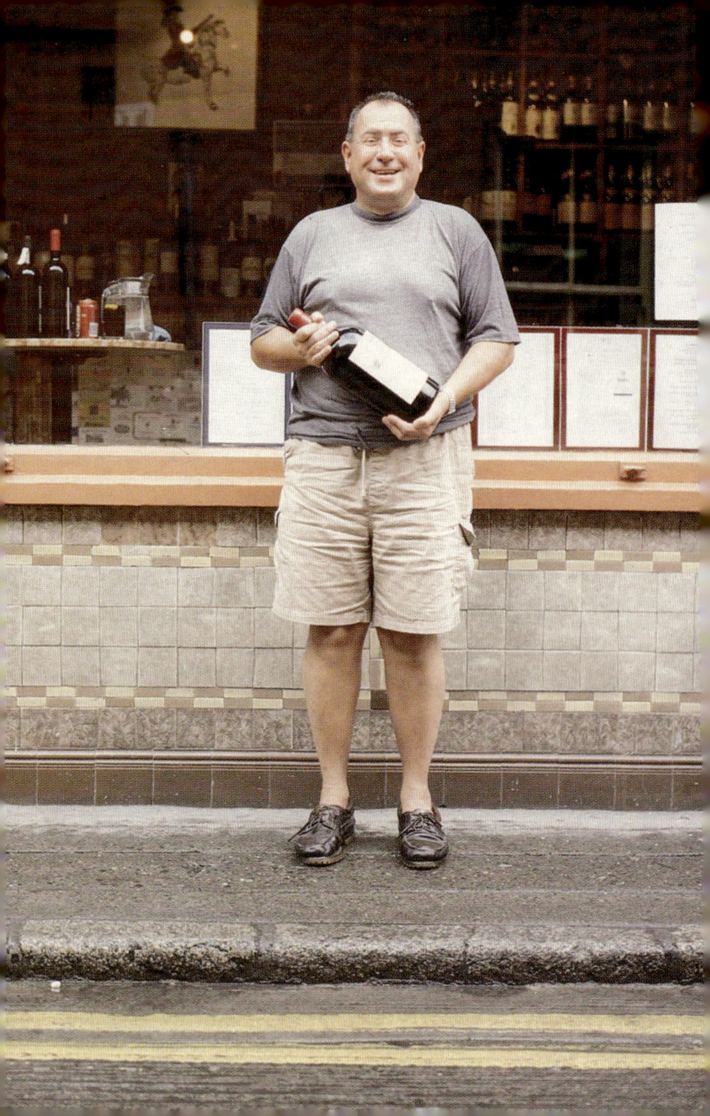

Il Primo

16 Montague Street
Dublin 2
t 478 3373

It has been a dramatic year on Montague Street. A little sandwich place called the Milk Bar is blossoming. The Montague Brasserie closed down. And a new restaurant space lies empty beside Dieter Bergmann's Italian café – proof that fingers were burned in 2003, and grand ambitions thwarted. Calling Il Primo a café is the first mistake here, because these aren't café prices. Dublin's most eccentric restaurateur (pictured on the left) has built a new dining room upstairs, and some of the staff have left – now replaced by the lovely Elaine and her gang from Moe's, another casualty of the sleeping tiger. All change, then? Not really. Anita Thoma's cooking is still very good and Il Primo is still one of the few restaurants in Ireland in which literally anything could happen. Besides, Dieter is such a priceless character that you almost feel lucky to have swelled his pockets.

Italian 2

Pearl

20 Merrion Street Upper
Dublin 2
t 661 3627 e info@pearl-brasserie.com
w www.pearl-brasserie.com

What sort of team would open a restaurant in the shadow of Patrick Guilbaud's two-star Michelin masterpiece? First you'd want a talented chef. Then you'd need pristine front of house. A lovely couple called Sebastian Masi and Kirsten Batt deserve to succeed in this poky basement spot. Sebastian was head chef in the Commons for five years, so he knows all about the perils of *haute cuisine*. He also worked for Monsieur Guilbaud. You can taste that pedigree in rich delights like the pan-fried duck foie gras, while at lunchtime, the Oyster Bar does a good range of platters-for-two of either cheeses, meats or fish for €18-€20. Now three years old, this moderately priced brasserie should stay the course. You may not like being in a basement, and the chilly modern decor is striking rather than elegant, but great service, attention to detail and damn good food all merit your business.

French

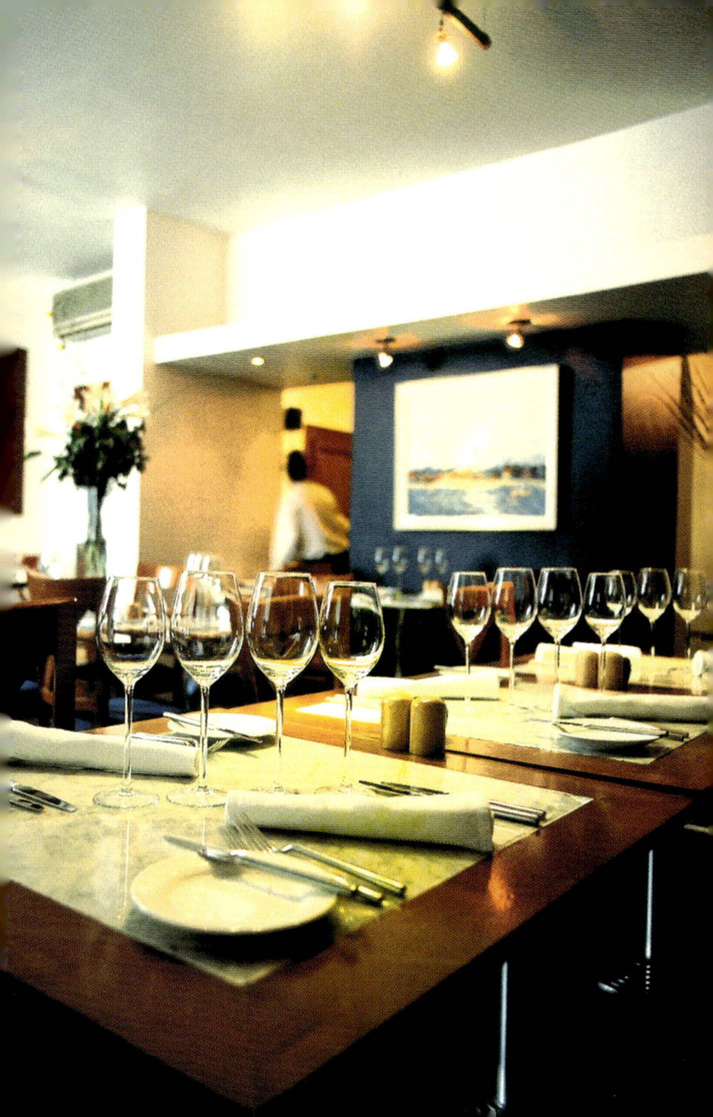

Ragazzi

109 Coliemore Road, Dalkey
County Dublin
t 284 7280

Cheap and cheerful, this Italian bistro is one of our favourite southsiders. Fabio and his team of flirty, olive-skinned Lotharios serve up the best pizzas in Dublin – extra thin and crispy, with the perfect topping-to-base ratio (from €10.50). They'll even put an egg on top. The menu has grown since our last visit – recent additions include a simple rocket & parmesan salad with fresh lemon juice and a generous buffalo mozzarella Caprese salad (€7.95). There's the usual choice of traditional pasta dishes (from €10.95) and veal scaloppinas – all fine . If you feel particularly unadventurous, stick to the pizzas and Italian beer and you can't go far wrong. Warning: the waiters fool around and throw a lot of shapes, so if you lack a sense of humour this probably isn't the place for you. Kid friendly and *very* blonde friendly.

CD Italian

The Red Bank

7 Church Street, Skerries
County Dublin
t 849 1005
w www.redbank.ie

Sit in the comfy reception area and have a Kir Royale with complimentary crudités, potato skins and periwinkles, while you check out the menu. The naff Irish interior is probably a hit with German tourists who buy David Hasselhoff records. There is nothing slick about the Red Bank. And that includes Terry McCoy, the "top TV seafood chef in Ireland." Razor fish/clams for starters were good, but the portion was huge and, like squid, they can be hard work. Dublin Bay prawns were simply cooked, served with butter and lemon. Spanking fresh sole with lemon and butter was heaven – plain and simple. Comprehensive wine list, but I wish they had more good white Burgundies. If you're travelling from the Southside, consider staying the night. The 12 new bedrooms are clean and matter-of-fact. Breakfast isn't bad either. Try the mushrooms fried in garlic butter, followed by the sole.

Seafood CD

Roly@The Pavilion

The Pavilion, Dun Laoghaire
Co Dublin
t 236 0286

Dun Laoghaire has become quite posh, with statue parks planned, organic farmers markets each Thursday and lots of restaurants. At dinner in Roly's last night – unrelated to Roly's old place in Ballsbridge, and *don't* ask why! – seared tuna with pickled cucumber and soy was way past rare, but tasty. Smoked salmon with potato salad, horseradish and crispy onions was far too full of spuds. But a roast rump of lamb with roasted veg was rustic, tasty and beautifully pink. Fillet of beef was smoky, flavoured up with truffle and celeriac mash. Ice creams were beautifully presented and obviously made in-house. Service is a lot smoother than it was last year, and despite the slick interiors, an older crowd seem to come here for romantic dinners *à deux*. There are tables outside, which should be smarter, and the loos still look like they belong in a hospital. But Roly remains a player.

CD Modern Irish

Roly's Bistro

7 Ballsbridge Terrace, Dublin 4
t 668 2611
w www.rolysbistro.ie

The RAI "Restaurant of the Year" is warm and inviting. Prices are reasonable, there's a good atmosphere and it's always packed. Sycophants compare Roly's to the Ivy in London – which would be accurate if the Ivy serviced every granny's day out in Leinster. Roly's is definitely not glamorous, and we often hear grumbles about the service. Paul Cartwright now runs the kitchen, giving Colin O'Daly some time to paint and pen recipes (his cook book is lovely). Great location, and at night there is plenty of parking along Herbert Park. The cooking is solid and unfussy, based around the principles of good, hearty bistro food. Try the duck wontons with cucumber and scallion salad (€9.95) and follow them with Dublin Bay prawns in garlic, lemon and parsley butter (€26.25). One of us still loves the first proper Irish bistro. The other thinks Roly's is a bit tired.

Modern Irish 4

Romano's

12 Capel Street
Dublin 1
t 872 6868

The frightful décor marks this out as a mid-week kind of place rather than a blow-out romantic Italian. The walls are half-pink, half-stripey, which, combined with the ornate white chairs and lighting as bright as an Arctic summer, makes Romano's look like an ersatz ice-cream parlour. So it's light on finesse – but similarly light on the pocket. Pasta and pizzas are around the €11 mark, a carafe of house red is €10, and starters begin at €5. Expect the staples: Margarita, Carbonara, Bolognaise and Matriciana. But the pastas are both organic and home-made. This isn't merely "fresh pasta" in inverted commas. If you like the Steps of Rome or Bar Italia, you're going to love Romano's, which is short on frills and long on value. Getting a full voltage smile when we said thank-you to the waitress made a nice alternative to the standard-issue surliness too.

Italian

Rubicon

6 Merrion Row
Dublin 2
t 676 5955

How many times have we passed this place and said "Bless"? It must be hard to have glitzy neighbours like Bang, the Unicorn and Pearl (not to mention the Merrion), but the last time we ate here, our party was large and the food was pretty good. Think casual: Irish grub gone global (there's that word again). The restaurant was clean and pleasant, busy without seeming PR princess-hysterical. For starters, try smoked salmon with sweet potato and sesame cake (€9.20), or ricotta, spinach and red onion tart with pine nuts (€8.95). Proceed to cod with Parma ham, gnocchi and crab claws (€21.95), or the braised lamb with caramelised leek and spring onion mash (€21.50). Vegetarians are well looked after, the location is handy and you will not meet a small army of social climbers.

Modern Irish

Shanahan's on the Green

119 St Stephen's Green
Dublin 2
t 407 0939 e sales@shanahans.ie
w www.shanahans.ie

We spend more time in Shanahan's than any other restaurant. How can we pretend this review will be fair? With that in mind: Meet Kevin. He's the sort of bartender who makes you feel like you're watching a particularly good film noir. Also makes the city's best Bloody Mary. If you haven't booked and there isn't a table free, don't worry. You can eat in the bar; handsome, clubby, deeply comfortable. Ask for Amanda. Avoid starters. Your little belly has no room for them – even resist the garlic prawns and John Shanahan's famous pea soup. Instead, order a fillet steak with all the trimmings; spinach, world's biggest onion rings and creamy mashed potato. Request a small bowl of creamed horseradish (*not* fresh horseradish). Devour, sit back and look at your date. You are now smiling at each other like a couple of lovesick teenagers. You haven't the energy to talk. You are paying silent homage to Shanahan's on the Green. It's all good.

2 Formal

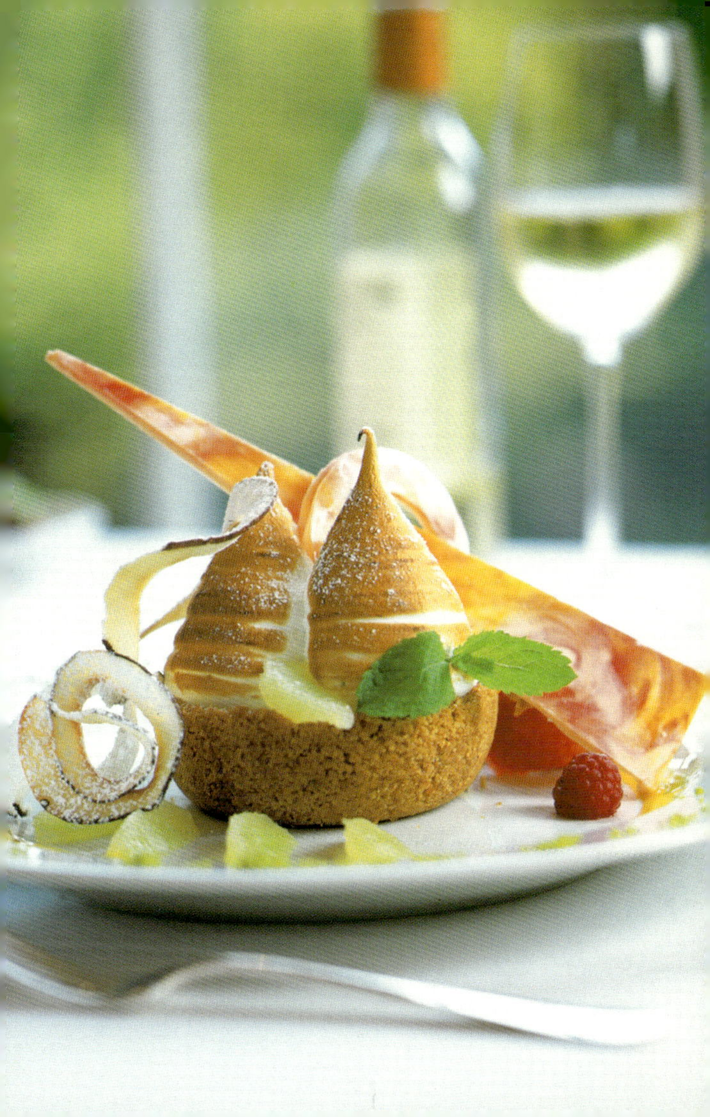

The Shelbourne Meridien

27 St Stephens Green, Dublin 2
t 676 6471
w www.lemeridien-hotel.com

There are two events in the Dublin calendar that belong to the Shelbourne Hotel. The first is the Trinity Ball – or rather, the hours *before* the Trinity Ball. Hundreds of students saunter into the Lord Mayor's Lounge for cocktails and gossip, in a scene that F Scott Fitzgerald would savour. The second is Christmas Eve, when Bono and anyone who has ever said "I know Bono" queues up to get in for a drink. Head barman Sean Boyd treats everyone with the same equanimity. We love taking visitors into the main dining room for breakfast – a classic Irish spread – and the Side Door serves a good smoked haddock lasagne for lunch. Back to that Lord Mayor's Lounge, where later in the afternoon you will hear beautiful piano music and see culchies, bankrupts and local legends like Ulick O'Connor. Over a slap-up afternoon tea, they indulge in a once-great Irish art. It is called conversation, and there is no better place for it.

2 Traditional Irish

Siam Thai

Sweepstake Centre, Ballsbridge
Dublin 4
t 660 1527
w www.siamthai.ie

This big and boring ground floor unit started life as an Asian restaurant. Then it became Brubecks, the Quaglino's of Dublin, and then it was Coopers. It was all a bit "Oops, I did it again." Siam Thai looks set to last a little longer than its predecessors, which is faint praise indeed. We were served by super-efficient women in gold brocade waiting dresses – with saucy slits up the side. It is a real in-and-out job... or else stay and get locked. We had some very good tom yung gai soup, plus some do-able satay followed by a tasty beef dish with black pepper and onion and a Thai beef salad. Efficient, clean and friendly. Deserves to do well in D4. By the way, owner Damon Crowe has now installed another Siam Thai in what used to be QV2, and he has grand plans to become a gourmet mogul of sorts. Watch this space.

Thai 4

Steps of Rome

Unit 1, Chatham Street
Dublin 2
t 670 5630

Welcome to John Carney country: fashionable young film-makers drink too much coffee here, when deadlines loom and ideas run dry. John loves this pokey Italian caff – hence it starred in *Bachelor's Walk*. We like the pizza slices, which are available to take away in brown paper bags that ooze with grease unless you start munching straight away. Some of the staff can be bloody rude. Mind you, the kitchen porter speaks good English. On a bad day, you may have to point at what you want, fight with other customers for a seat and leg it down to the Westbury to spend a penny. Beware of the red wine. It has been sitting under hot lights for too long and can be positively frizzante. Instead, order lots of Italian beer and stick to the pizza: our favourite is the potato and rosemary one.

Cheap & Cheerful

The Still Room

Old Jameson Distillery, Bow Street
Dublin 7
t 807 2355 e reservations@ojd.ie

Don't be put off by Smithfield's burgeoning reputation as the capital of shabby chic Dublin – and yes, we know it's still more shabby than chic. This inviting café in the old Jameson distillery is surprisingly good. Classic Irish comfort-food like bacon with parsley sauce, served with cabbage and new potatoes (€7.25-€10), or roast rib of beef with wholegrain mustard seed (€7.25-€10), and tea time staples are offered at reasonable prices in an area that badly needs more decent eateries. It's not particularly healthy fare, but what is anymore? As Edgar Howe put it, "The better a pie tastes, the worse it is for you." Anyway, in the Still Room you will see jolly Americans and tribunal-rich barristers out for short, boozy lunches. Have a shot and scale the adjoining chimney at Chief O'Neill's hotel, which offers an astonishing view of the city.

Traditional Irish 7

La Stampa

35 Dawson Street
Dublin 2
t *671 7113* **e** *dine@lastampa.ie*
w *www.lastampa.ie*

Nietzsche said that bad cooks have delayed human development longest and impaired it most. Of course, Nietzsche spent the last ten years of his life in a mental asylum. Bad cooks are certainly responsible for the food at La Stampa down the years. Things have recently picked up in the kitchen, and at last the food is beginning to do justice to Dublin's most beautiful dining room. We love the smoked haddock risotto starter (€13.50) and think the roast rib of beef is a complete rip-off at €34.50. Louis Murray has now added bedrooms upstairs for particularly sleepy/horny diners, and there's a Thai restaurant downstairs called Tiger Becks, which we raved about last year. How wrong we were. A mixed bag then, and don't forget the 10% service charge, automatically added to your bill. If your waiter is lazy, incompetent or stupid, don't hesitate to tell him your opinion of automatic service charges.

Italian

The Trocadero

3/4 St Andrew's Street
Dublin 2
t 677 5545

There is no point amending our comments about the Trocadero, which is one of those restaurants you visit religiously – or not at all. Despite a recent makeover, it still has an eighties buzz. Those Tony Bennett tunes and the actors' headshots which line the walls of this showbiz favourite lend it a timeless twang. Maitre d' Robert Doggett still runs the show with good humour and great courtesy. Head chef Joseph Murray churns out comfort food – big racks of lamb (€23.49) and a reliable fillet steak (€21.52) – for bitchy actors ("I slept with that prick") who know little about life off-stage. Ignore them with all the haughtiness you can muster. Loudly drop names like 'Pearson' and 'Stembridge.' One of the few restaurants in this city in which you are guaranteed a memorable evening – even if the food is erratic, to put it mildly.

Traditional Irish 2

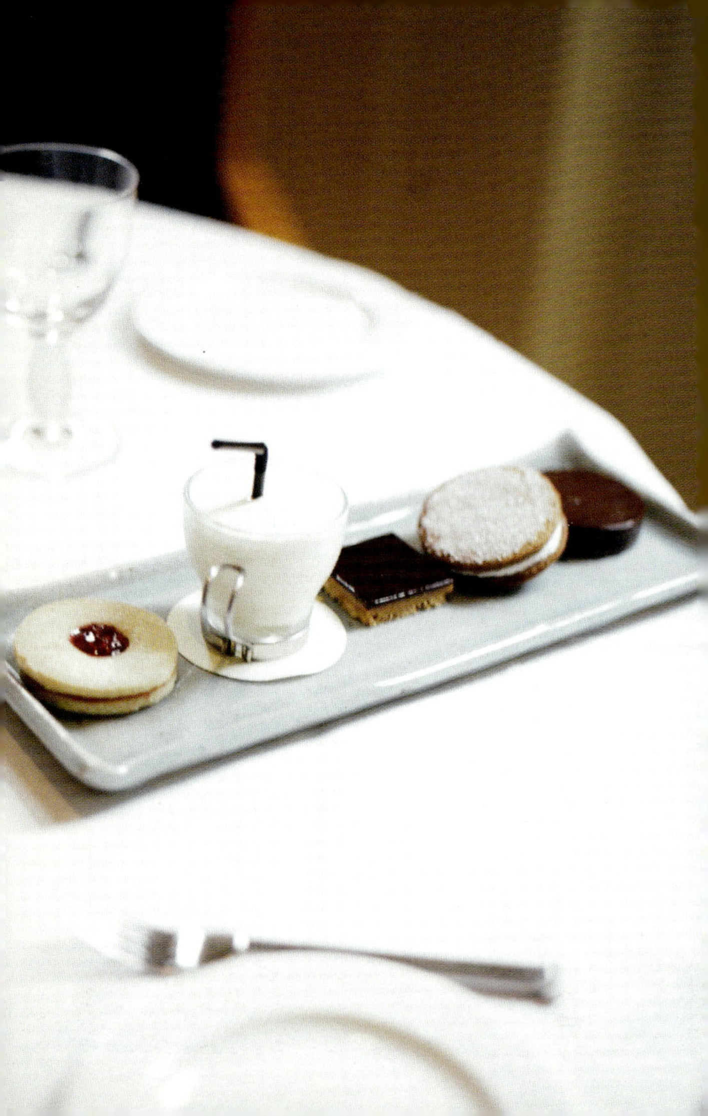

The Tea Room

The Clarence Hotel, 6-8 Wellington Quay
Dublin 2
t 407 0813
w www.theclarence.ie

This restaurant should be busier – end of story. Anthony Ely's cooking and smooth service under Nick Meunier (a former Marco Pierre White man) are reason enough to eat here all the time. But they *still* haven't removed the banquette that splits the room in two. We often beg the genial GM, Robert Van Eerde, to beg his boss, one Bono, to throw it out (yes, we are obsessed). In the meantime, well-heeled visitors and savvy locals flock to what could be one of the nicest dining rooms in our guide. Elsewhere in the same hotel, the Octagon bar is the perfect place to meet for cocktails. Facilities like valet-parking and guaranteed star-gazing lend further charm. Downside? Leave by the back entrance and the horror of being in Temple Bar can give you indigestion. On the plus side, seeing all those hideous hen parties may put you off marriage (and therefore divorce) forever.

Formal 2

Thornton's

128 St Stephen's Green
Dublin 2
t*478 7008*

We put Kevin Thornton on the cover of *The Dubliner* when he opened this restaurant. Abandoning Portobello was a bold move for the man whom Helen Lucy Burke calls "the best chef in the city." Thornton didn't lose either of his stars when he made the move, a vote of confidence from the boring Michelin men that is not exactly echoed by punters. You will often share the large dining room with more staff (*magnificent* staff) than customers. It's a desperate sight, only relieved by food so good that silence suits your palate: to appreciate it, you need to concentrate on Thornton's classical French cuisine. You also need to fork out, big time. There are plenty of people who resent such impositions. But go, dammit, and do your bit to support this extraordinary project. It may not last forever.
P.S. One of us won't set foot in the place – "which is nothing," says Domini, "to do with the fact that I'm barred."

2 Formal

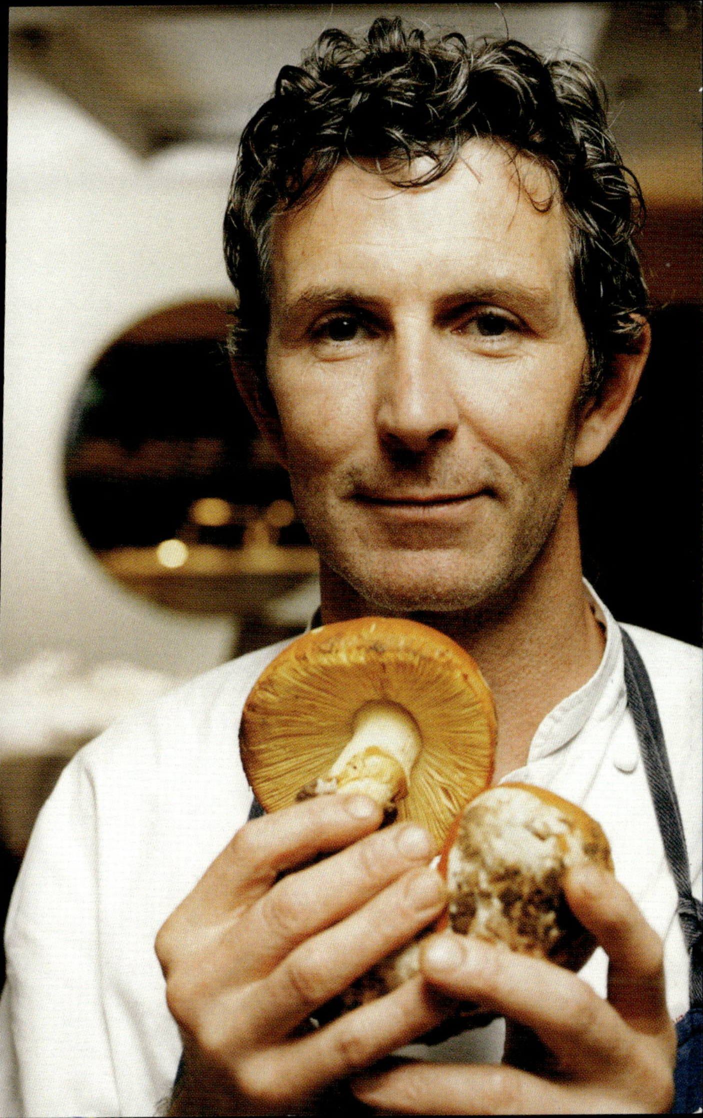

The Unicorn

12b Merrion Court
Dublin 2
℡ 676 2182

With his endless supply of compliments for well-heeled dames and a warm welcome for everyone else, it is probably safe to say that Giorgio Casari is the most charming man in the Irish restaurant business. We have both had stand-up rows with him in the last six months. Giorgio was hopping mad with us for daring to criticise the food in the Unicorn. In fairness, it has now improved. We like to think Giorgio gave his staff a kick in the arse after we said that Dublin's most glamorous restaurant was all too typical of the city today: lots of style, *no substance*. You certainly get that impression when you look around the room. At lunch, regulars stick to the antipasto. At dinner, have meatballs and polenta, calamari or fritto misto. If you want to spot people who are famous in Ireland and nowhere else, you will love the Unicorn. It is Dublin's (rather provincial) answer to the Ivy in London and Le Cirque in New York.

Italian

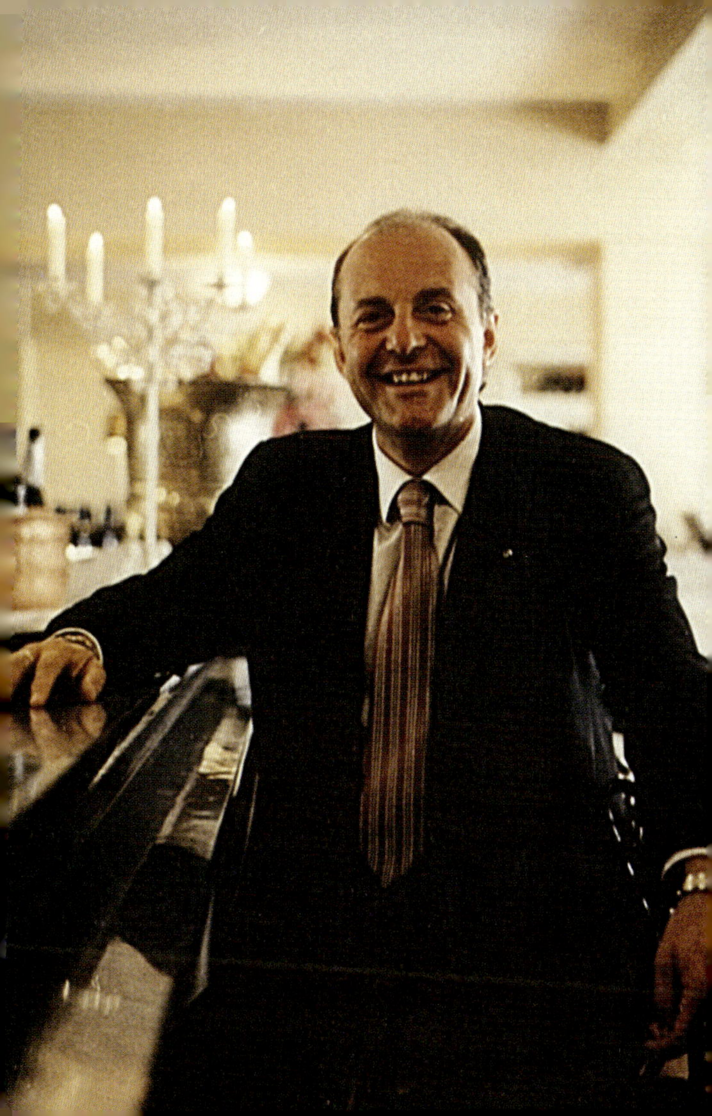

The Vaults

Harbour Master Place, IFSC
Dublin 1
t 605 4700
w www.thevaults.ie

Chefs often get involved in high-profile associations that are a bit like celebrity marriages. Initially, everyone couldn't be happier. Then, as tales of Mr Superstar running off with the pool-boy emerge, you realise that you have been conned at some level. Not here. Chef Michael Martin (ex-Tea Room) runs this vast pub under Connolly Station in the IFSC. It's all stone, leather and plasma screens – quite chic for what is essentially a posh bar. Chicken wings, open sandwiches, pizza and burgers are all well above standard pub fare. The weekend Kids Club provides a large, clean space for you to have lunch in, without torturing other diners (there is face-painting and Rug-Rat stuff to distract the critters). Does this encourage parents to get sloshed and drive the kids home drunk? Nope. People come here for good food in a casual environment. What they get up to on a Saturday night is a different story.

1 World

Vermillion

94 Terenure Road North, Terenure
Dublin 6W
t 499 1400

The smartest bathrooms in a Dublin restaurant are above a pub in Terenure. Jerry Kochanski spent a fortune on this place, and although manager Nisheeth Tak has left, the Irishman still seems determined to make a go of it. Vermillion is the only Indian restaurant in the city that feels contemporary, and when it's busy, the dining room has real energy and ambience. Ignore the main courses, which have less spice than Val Joyce. Order loads of starters, which are snappy and tasty. Try eral sukka, jumbo prawns tossed in garlic and yoghurt (€8.50). Gorgeous naan bread too. There is a decent kids' menu, as well as symbols for low-fat, plain and hot dishes to help you make a smart choice. Good value wine list too. Altogether, a pleasant experience with excellent service – despite the grim location.

Indian 6

Yamamori

71 South Great George's Street
Dublin 2
t 475 5001

Loud, fun and utterly formulaic, this evergreen Japanese offers all the usual sushi and sashimi fare at reasonable prices. Big groups will appreciate the raucous, laid-back atmosphere but couples might find noise levels rather too threatening. Staff are very much cooler than you or I will ever be. On the plus side, portions are big. If you like norimaki, stick to the avocado and pickled vegetables. Best dish? Chilli beef ramen (€14.50). Beware: the bill mounts up when you order a couple of side-dishes, but they're half the fun. Gyoza (€6.50) and deep-fried king prawns (€7.50) disappear particularly fast. Desserts confirm that Yamamori is more fun than authentic – American cheese cake, fruit crumble and crème caramel – but we're not complaining. Several gallons of hot sake will make you feel like Tokyo Joe.

2 Japanese

Zuccini

47 Ranelagh Village
Dublin 6
t 497 8655

Given the number of places that close within a year of opening, it seems like grand folly to recommend a restaurant that is brand new. But we do like Zuccini, despite its many flaws. Firstly, the descriptions on the menu suggest *haute cuisine*. The prices confirm that impression (to be fair, this is Ranelagh, darling). The room itself is far too cramped to justify the prices, the noise levels are very high and the lack of table-cloths did *not* please mum. Don't come here for a relaxing night out – or indeed on a date, as your neighbours are bound to hear everything you say (if you think 'so what?' you belong on *Big Brother*). But Zuccini is great fun; the customers are all rich, good-looking people who pretend to vote Labour, the atmosphere is upbeat, the staff are lovely and the food is okay. Best dishes on the night were roast chicken with a lovely truffle mash (€19.50) and the halibut special.

Modern European | 6

Index

Dublin 1

101 Talbot	6
Alilang	8
Bangkok Café	17
Chapter One	38
D One Restaurant	44
Halo at The Morrison	68
Romano	114
The Vault	130

Dublin 2

Ar Vicoletto	12
Avoca	10
Aya	13
Baccaro, Il	14
Bad Ass Café	15
Bang	16
Bistro, The	23
Bleu Bistro	24
Brownes Brasserie	29
Café Bar Deli	30
Captain Americas	31
Cave, La	32
Cedar Tree, The	34
Cellar, The	36
Chai Yo	37
Chili Club, The	40
Corte, La	43
Dish	48
Dobbins Wine Bistro	50
Dunne and Crescenzi	51
L'Ecrivain	52
Eden Restaurant	53
Elephant and Castle	54
Ely	55
Exchange, The	58
Fitzers	59
Fréres Jacques, Les	61
Govinda's	66
Gruel	67
Kevin Arundel at Number Ten	75
Kilkenny Centre Café	73
Maison des Gourmets, La	83
Mao	84
Mère Zou, La	85
Mermaid, The	86
Milano	87
Montys of Kathmandu	88
Old Stand, The	95
One Pico	98
Papaya	101
Patrick Guilbaud	102
Pearl	108
Posto, Il	105
Primo, Il	107
Rubicon	115
Shanahan's on the Green	116
Shelbourne Meridien, The	118
Stampa, La	122
Steps of Rome	120
Tea Room, The	125
Thornton's	126
Trocadero, The	123

Unicorn, The	128	Havana Tapas Bar		71
Yamamori	132	Locks		82
Dublin 3		*Dublin 14*		
Kinara	76	Olive Tree, The		96
Dublin 4		*Dublin 18*		
Berkeley Room	19	Bistro One		22
Ernie's	56	Gables, The		65
French Paradox	62			
Four Seasons	60	*County Dublin*		
Furama	64	Aqua		9
O'Connells	90	Beaufield Mews		18
Ocean	92	Bon Appetit		25
Roly's Bistro	113	Cavistons		33
Siam Thai	119	China-Sichuan		39
		Da Roberto		46
Dublin 6		Dali's		47
Bijou	20	Jaipur		72
Vermillion	131	King Sitric		78
Zucchini	133	Kish		81
		Nosh		89
Dublin 7		Old Schoolhouse, The		93
Hanley at the Bar	70	Osborne, The		99
Still Room, The	121	PD's Woodhouse		104
		Ragazzi		110
Dublin 8		Red Bank, The		111
Brewery Bar, The	26	Roly@The Pavilion		112

Cheap & Cheerful	*Indian*	*Modern European*	*Spanish*
Chinese	*Italian*	*Modern Irish*	*Thai*
Formal	*Japanese*	*Nepalese*	*Traditional Irish*
French	*Lebanese*	*Seafood*	*World*

- **6** 101 Talbot
- **8** Alilang
- **10** Avoca
- **12** ArVicoletto
- **13** Aya
- **14** Baccaro, Il
- **15** Bad Ass Café
- **16** Bang
- **17** Bangkok Café
- **23** Bistro, The
- **24** Bleu Bistro
- **26** Brewery Bar, The
- **29** Brownes Brasserie
- **30** Café Bar Deli
- **31** Captain Americas
- **32** Cave, La
- **34** Cedar Tree, The
- **36** Cellar, The
- **37** Chai Yo
- **38** Chapter One
- **40** Chili Club, The
- **43** Corte, La
- **44** D One
- **48** Dish
- **50** Dobbins Wine Bistro
- **51** Dunne and Crescenzi
- **52** L'Ecrivain
- **53** Eden
- **54** Elephant & Castle
- **55** Ely
- **58** Exchange, The
- **59** Fitzers
- **61** Fréres Jacques, Les
- **66** Govinda's
- **67** Gruel
- **68** Halo at The Morrison
- **70** Hanley @the Bar
- **71** Havana
- **73** Kilkenny Centre Café
- **75** Kevin Arundel at Number Ten
- **83** Maison des Gourmets, La
- **84** Mao
- **85** Mère Zou, La
- **86** Mermaid, The
- **87** Milano
- **88** Montys of Kathmandu
- **92** Ocean
- **95** Old Stand, The
- **98** One Pico
- **101** Papaya
- **102** Patrick Guilbaud
- **105** Posto, Il
- **107** Primo, Il
- **108** Pearl
- **114** Romano
- **115** Rubicon
- **116** Shanahan's
- **118** Shelbourne Meridien, The
- **120** Steps of Rome, The
- **121** The Still Room
- **122** La Stampa
- **123** Trocadero, The
- **125** Tea Room, The
- **126** Thornton's
- **128** Unicorn, The
- **130** The Vaults
- **132** Yamamori

Map of Dublin City Centre

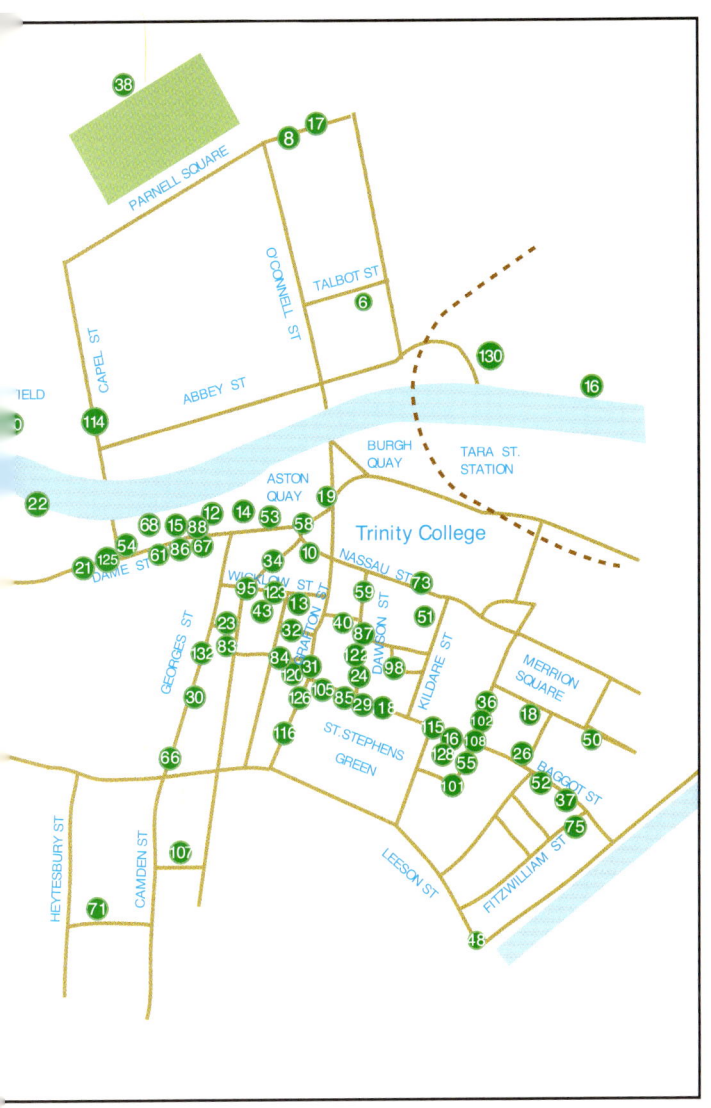

Streets and Locations:

- Parnell Square (38)
- O'Connell St
- Capel St
- Talbot St (8, 17, 6)
- Abbey St (114)
- Burgh Quay
- Tara St. Station (130, 16)
- Aston Quay (22)
- Dame St (21, 125, 54, 61, 86, 67, 68, 15, 88, 12, 14, 53, 58, 19)
- Wicklow St (34, 10, 95, 43, 23, 132, 83)
- Nassau St (73)
- Trinity College
- Grafton St (13, 32, 123, 40, 59, 87, 51)
- Dawson St (24, 122, 98, 31, 84, 120, 126, 105, 85, 29, 18, 115)
- Kildare St (36, 102, 18)
- Merrion Square (50)
- Georges St (30, 66)
- St. Stephens Green (116, 128, 16, 108, 55, 101)
- Baggot St (26, 52, 37)
- Fitzwilliam St (75)
- Heytesbury St (71)
- Camden St (107)
- Leeson St (48)

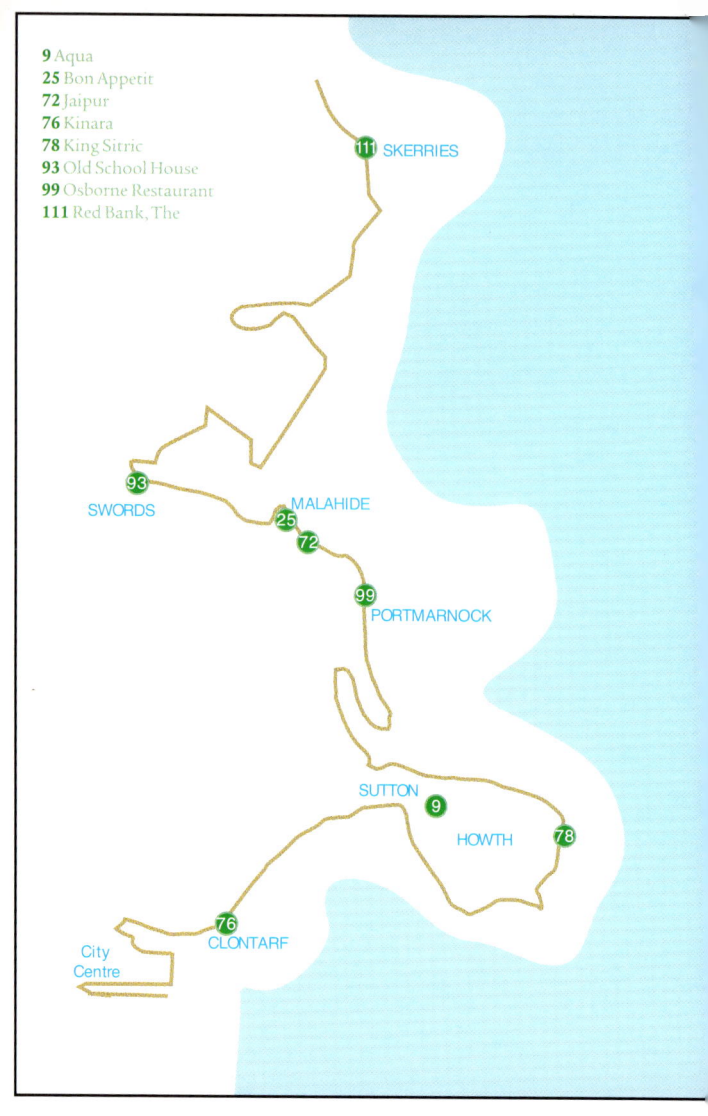

9 Aqua
25 Bon Appetit
72 Jaipur
76 Kinara
78 King Sitric
93 Old School House
99 Osborne Restaurant
111 Red Bank, The

SKERRIES
SWORDS
MALAHIDE
PORTMARNOCK
SUTTON
HOWTH
CLONTARF
City Centre

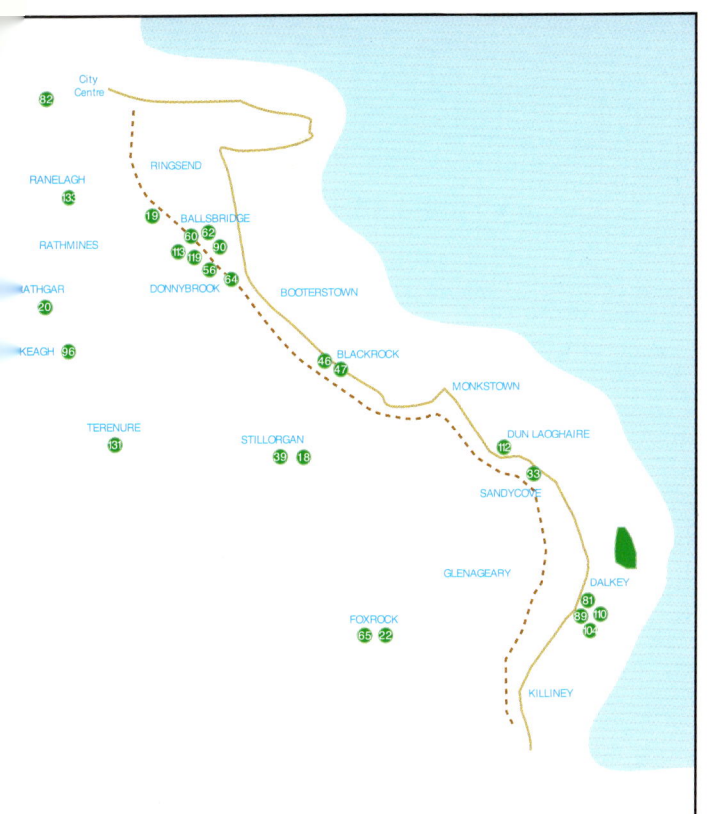

18 Beaufield Mews
19 Berkeley Room
20 Bijou
22 Bistro One
33 Caviston's
39 China-Sichuan
46 Da Roberto
47 Dali's
56 Ernie's

60 The Four Seasons
62 French Paradox
64 Furama
65 Gables, The
81 Kish
82 Locks
89 Nosh
90 O'Connells
96 Olive Tree, The

104 PD's Woodhouse
110 Ragazzi
112 Roly@The Pavilion
113 Roly's Bistro
119 Siam Thai
131 Vermillion
133 Zuccini

Acknowledgements

The authors wish to acknowledge the assistance and support of Fergal Downey of Gilbeys and Leo Moore of Diageo. We are delighted to have Santa Rita Wines as our new sponsor for the book. Thank you.

We are greatly indebted to the staff of *The Dubliner* magazine, in particular to the editor Emily Hourican, and to the Art Director Joanne Murphy, whose photographs are used throughout. Joanne also designed the book, which has been widely complimented for its utility and elegance.

Thank you, also, to those journalists who wrote restaurant reviews for us over the last year, including Helen Lucy Burke, John Brereton, Tara Murphy, Quentin Fottrell, Liam Campbell, Brendan O'Connor, Anne Iremonger, Bridget Hourican, Paul Trainer, Jennifer Powell and Annaick Farrell.

Finally, thanks to Aillil and Deirdre O'Reilly for proof-reading the book, and also to Fintan Taite, who designed the symbols.